At the Table with

LBJ and Lady Bird

TEXAS WILDFLOWERS
BLUEBONNET
Lupinus texensis

GIANT SPIDERWORT
Tradescantia gigantea

Indian Blanket
Gaillardia pulchella

J.S.

Indian Paintbrush
Castilleja indivisa

Purple Coneflower
Echinacea purpurea

At the Table with

LBJ and Lady Bird: History, Humor, and True Texas Recipes

Written and Illustrated by

Jean E. Schuler

TCU Press

Fort Worth, Texas

TCU Box 298300
Fort Worth, Texas 76129
To order books: 1.800.826.8911

Design by Bill Brammer

I dedicate this book- and the 10,000 hours spent in
researching, drawing, reading books about LBJ, allowing
life to happen and still finishing it- to my very
talented nephew Spencer Flynn. He has the courage and the
fight to pursue his talent of acting, making music, and
accepting that his soul runs his body. Many people think
we have a body with a soul, but truth be told it is the
other way around. Mostly creative people know that.
Hats off to you, Spencer, and may you have BIG success.
Just listen to your soul. It will take you to the moon
and back. I Love you so much!

Thank you Ann Saxton-Volkwein. You met me at a coffee
house on a cold, wet, rainy day in January, listened
to my idea of compiling LBJ recipes, said it was a great
idea, and GO for it! (Only later did I find out she worked
with Guy Fieri in producing his books.)

So much help came from the archivist at the LBJ Presidential
Library. Every one of you is a huge blessing. Thank you so,
so much. Tina Houston, you signed my research card granting
me the privilege of researching in the incredible library.
Laura Eggert, you are a great Volunteer Director. I have
learned so much history from you. Anne Wheeler, Communications
Director, thank you for ideas and for promoting the recipe
cards. To my fellow volunteers, you make the museum a great
place to visit. Thank you Sherry Brown for supporting
my creative side.

California friends that baked cookies and tested dishes,
you totally rock! Thank you Alma Ronis And the whole Ainley
Family for your support. A big thanks to my seasoned writer
friend, Joloyn Wilde in the U.K. for his business sense.
You said do this and don't do that. And you were right!

Rosie James, Jennifer Vail, Molly and Randal Housey, Ann
Hughes, Leslie Mashburn, Tribble's, Chris Eve, Forrest,
Buda and Logan Dunlap, Bill Naddeff, Elizabeth Cubberly
Tracy, Mayor Hardy, Lisa Beall, Don, Julie and A.B. Judson,
Whitney Temple (The big motivator). Taylor Kidd, Darin
Shus, Deborah Brobeck, Dennis, Mark and Mel, Mia Singletary,
Addie Boyles, Sheena and Gary Christie, thank you very
much for your support. You kept asking me about "the book",
so I didn't quit.

Thank you to my family that ate the testing food, as I
called it. Steve, Joan, Elizabeth, James, Catherine and
Annie. John, Rachel, Lauren, Jennifer and Michelle, you
might not know it but you ate "testing food". Jane, Preston,
Spencer, Morgan and Larry, Thank you. The Allen family-
Wilson, Wilson, R, Janet, Amelia and Channing, I think you
might of missed being a tester, but I love you just the same!.

Mom, thank you for being my assistant in the kitchen and
blessing me with three awesome sisters and one nice bro"

And saving the very best for last is my team at TCU Press.
To Kathy Walton, the very talented editor; she worked
endless hours and absolute magic in turning my pile of
paper into a book. Truly she is a magician! Dan Williams,
Molly Spain, Rebecca Allen and James Lehr this book would
not have made it without your efforts behind the scene.
I can't thank you enough for your hard-work and dedication.

—J. E. S.
May 2022

Contents

Foreword

When I first started writing about food for the *Austin American-Statesman*, I learned about the repository of Lady Bird recipes housed at the LBJ Presidential Library and about Zephyr Wright, the longtime Johnson family cook who famously moved to the White House to continue cooking for the president and the women he affectionately called his "three girls."

Although there's no doubt that the president and Lady Bird loved hosting barbecues, state dinners, and large family meals, Zephyr was behind that fresh-baked spoonbread. The way to LBJ's heart was through his stomach, so he developed a close relationship with Zephyr and her husband, Sammy, who was the family's driver. They would tell him about the discrimination they faced outside the workplace, and many sources point to their relationship as one reason he decided to sign the Civil Rights Act of 1964. She was on hand when he signed that historic piece of legislation, and he gave her one of the pens, famously saying that she deserved it more than he did.

Jean Schuler's connection to the Johnson family started with a chance encounter when she crossed paths with the couple on their ranch in 1971. She wrote LBJ a letter. He wrote her back. She never forgot it.

Many years later, while volunteering at the presidential library on the University of Texas campus, Schuler tracked down that letter with an archivist. Seeing her eleven-year-old handwriting transported her back to that era, when KFC served chicken in buckets and LBJ was still taking people on what they thought was a joyride in that blue Amphicar along the Pedernales River—until Johnson would yell out, "no brakes, no brakes," then head right into the river.

What a brilliant idea Schuler had to pair those archival recipes with her own free-hand illustrations. Her whimsical doodles of biscuits, pies, cakes, Raisin Bran boxes, classic Texas barbecue, and those buckets of fried chicken offer a new lens to view this historic family and this historic time in American history.

Even before taking office, LBJ and Lady Bird hosted epic dinner parties, where people of different political persuasions could come together to both argue and be merry. After particularly hard days, the family found comfort in familiar dishes that they'd been eating for a long time. On the easier days, food would be at the centerpiece of the celebration.

LBJ led the country during a tumultuous era, and as we live through another unprecedented time, *At the Table with LBJ and Lady Bird: History, Humor, and True Texas Recipes* made me think about what we can learn from the Johnsons as we find our own way through what can feel like never-ending uncertainty.

Zephyr's life—and possibly the course of the entire country—changed when she met the Johnsons way back in the early 1940s, when Lady Bird and LBJ were many years into trying to start a family and weren't sure if they'd ever have children.

Schuler's life changed the day she saw the president and his wife and later received a letter in the mail. A letter that made her feel special all over again when she found it more than fifty years later.

The people who come into our lives during tough and tender times often have an outsized influence on our lives. LBJ was one of those people. The archivist who led Jean Schuler to the archives at the LBJ Library the day that old letter was found also falls on that list. Whose lives will change when they read these stories and think about the Johnson family or their own lives in a new way? That's the legacy of kindness and dedication that LBJ and Lady Bird would have loved to see.

Addie Broyles
June 2022

Addie Broyles is an Austin-based writer, quilter, and tarot card reader. She was the food writer at the *Austin American-Statesman* from 2008 to 2021, and she now writes her weekly column at **thefeministkitchen.com**.

Preface

I get a lot of questions about why I wrote this collection of stories and recipes. Well, here goes. I am a volunteer at the front desk of the LBJ Presidential Museum in Austin, Texas. I love meeting people from all over the world and love learning about history. LBJ is as big as Texas history, as it turns out. He took every minute, every second God gave him and used it, mostly for the good of you and me.

A couple of things happened that got me researching what LBJ and Lady Bird ate, what they had their chef prepare for State Dinners, and what they liked to eat day in, day out.

I read that Lady Bird liked to share the Texas ranch recipes she'd collected for years with her personal cook at the White House, Zephyr Wright. LBJ loved real Texas food. Barbecue was a big deal at his Texas White House parties. I got curious about the recipes. I love reading cookbooks. But guess what??? There was no LBJ cookbook. What? Such an interesting couple, so many events, and no cookbook. Checking in the museum store, I found a postcard with the famous Pedernales Chili recipe on it, and a few other things, but that was it. When I asked an archivist at the library, she said there were recipes I could look at in the research library on the tenth floor. I think when she told me that a sliver of Luci Johnson's wedding cake was in a file, I had to see for myself. I also asked the archivist what all did the president save? And she replied, "A lot. Almost everything. There are over forty million pieces of paper saved." Hmmm. "Well," I continued, "I wonder if my letter to President Johnson was saved?"

"Oh!" she exclaimed. "When did you write it?"

"About...forty-five years ago. I was eleven years old. I saw Lady Bird and him at the ranch. I was standing on the side of a dirt road in the LBJ Historical Park, looking at longhorn cattle, and out of a dust cloud appeared LBJ and Lady Bird in a big old Lincoln, going right past us. LBJ tipped his Stetson hat and looked right at us."

She said, "Just a minute," and walked off. Twenty minutes later she reappeared with my letter. I immediately recognized my stationery. It was my "special" stationery, only used to write my grandmothers or something very important. I have included a copy of it here, along with my engraving of the ranch and the sweet letter I received in the mail.

I felt connected to the library at this point. After all, my letter was part of presidential history! I made an appointment with the archivist to discuss researching recipes. She approved, and I received my official research card.

From that moment on I have been researching, reading about LBJ parties, or testing recipes. I love it!

Dear, Mr. Johnson
    My name is Jean Schuler
    I live in Austin. I am 11yrs. old.
  I was thrilled Sunday. I saw
you in you green ford.
You are a smart lucky man.
You have beautiful land, Longhorns
and a beautiful house. I've
see you're birthplace.
              P.S. write me
              I'll have something
              to brage about

your a lucky
man Mr. Johnson.   Jean Schuler

      Good Grief

This is how it all started. A letter making me feel special.
I never forgot the letters <u>LBJ.</u>

AUSTIN, TEXAS

Dear Jean:

This engraving of the ranch is sent as a
little souvenir of your visit out our way
and as a small thank you for a nice letter.
I <u>am</u> lucky and more so today because you
to<u>ok</u> the time to write me as you did.

Sincerely,

Miss Jean Schuler

August 26, 1971

This is the engraving I received in the mail with the nice letter signed by LBJ. I remember the envelope was padded, and the engraving is on thick stock and embossed in gold. I was beside myself with joy!

LBJ Ranch

With best wishes

Lady Bird Johnson   Lyndon B. Johnson

LBJ and
Lady Bird

The marriage of Claudia Alta Taylor and Lyndon Baines Johnson

Wedding

On September 12, 1934, LBJ and Claudia Alta Taylor met. It was a whirlwind romance—LBJ was twenty-six and Lady Bird was just twenty-two years old. They met in the office of a mutual friend in Austin. LBJ had plans that evening, so he asked Lady Bird to breakfast. The "breakfast" date turned into a long event, as the couple spent the day driving around Austin.

"that is Lady Bird's real name."

LBJ EVEN PROPOSED!

In an oral history interview, Lady Bird recalled, "I do believe before the day was over, he did ask me to marry him, and I thought he was just out of his mind. It was very...well, I'm a slow, considered sort generally, and certainly not given to quick conclusions or much rash behavior."

Undeterred by her refusal, LBJ introduced her to his family the next day. And when he had to drive home to Washington, DC, where he worked as a congressional aide, he dropped Lady Bird off in her hometown of Karnack, Texas, and met her father.

While Lady Bird remained hesitant at the speed of the courtship, her father seemed to approve of her suitor. He remarked, "You've brought a lot of boys home, and this time you've brought a man."

On November 17, 1934, Johnson and Lady Bird drove to San Antonio to "commit matrimony," as she would later describe it. Although LBJ had given her an engagement ring, they had no wedding bands picked out. Lady Bird still had not made up her mind to marry Lyndon, but on the drive to San Antonio she agreed to get married. Dan Quill, a friend and postmaster of San Antonio, bought a wedding band at the nearby Sears and Roebuck for $2.50. They were married at St. Mark's Church in San Antonio, in front of a few of LBJ's friends.

They honeymooned in Xochimilco, Mexico. They were happily married for thirty-nine years, until LBJ passed away in 1973.

More facts about Lyndon Baines Johnson than most people
will ever know.

Full name: Lyndon Baines Johnson
Birthplace: Stonewall, Texas
Date of birth: August 27, 1908
Height: 6'3"
Weight: fluctuated between 195 and 220 lbs.
Hair color: Brown
Eye color: Brown
College graduated from: Southwest Texas State Teacher's
                        College (now Texas State University)
Sports played/watched: bowling, swimming, golf, horseback
                       riding, baseball (as a young man)
Watched: Football
Hobbies: dominos, touring the ranch

Favorite food(s) Fresca, tapioca, German chocolate cake,
peach cobbler, Mexican food, cornbread, chicken fried steak,
BBQ, melon, banana pudding, peach ice cream, coconut macaroon
cookies
Favorite books: nonfiction, biographies, topical books on
national and international problems.
Favorite songs and singers: "Raindrops Keep Falling on My Head,"
"Carolina Moon," "Anniversary Waltz," "Always," "America the
Beautiful," "Onward Christian Soldiers," "The Battle Hymn of the
Republic," Vienna waltzes, anything from Oklahoma, Camelot, The
Sound of Music, and Hello Dolly; Gene Autry and Charley Pride.
Favorite movies: Butch Cassidy and the Sundance Kid, Guess
Who's Coming to Dinner? The Searchers and other John Wayne
movies; James Bond movies.
—Had his tailor make his shirt sleeves too short to make his
short arms look longer. Wore Old Spice and enjoyed Gunsmoke.

LBJ died of a heart attack in 1973, four years after
leaving the office. Lady Bird was in a meeting when he
had the heart attack. By the time she got back to the
ranch he had passed away.

"Peace is a journey of a thousand miles

and it must be taken one step at a time."

        --Lyndon B. Johnson
        Thirty-sixth President of the United States

3

Claudia Alta Taylor

Lady Bird was born on December 22, 1912,
in Karnack, Texas. During her infancy
her nursemaid, Alice Tittle, said that
she was as

"PURTY AS A LADYBIRD"

it stuck!

Her father and siblings called her "Lady."
Her husband called her "Bird."
She used the name "Bird" on her driver's
license.

Lady Bird was largely raised by her aunt Effie
Pattillo. When Lady Bird was 5 years old her
mother fell down a flight of stairs while pregnant
and died of complications of a miscarriage.

She had two elder brothers, Thomas Jefferson Jr.
(1901-1959) and Antonio (1904-1986)
Her widowed father married twice more.

She developed her lifelong love of the
outdoors as a child growing up in the tall pines
and bayous of East Texas, where she watched the
WILDFLOWERS bloom each spring.

During her Senior year she realized she had the
highest grades in her class, she "purposely
allowed her grades to slip" so she would not
have to be the valedictorian or salutatorian or give
a speech.

After graduating from high school in May 1928,
Lady Bird went to University of Alabama for a
summer session, where she took her first journalism
class. She became homesick for TEXAS and did not
return for the Fall semester.

Hook- em!
HORNS!

Claudia Alta Taylor continued

Instead, she and a high school friend enrolled
at St. Mary's Episcopal College for Women.

After graduatingfrom St. Mary's in 1930 she went
to Austin with a friend from Marshall. She
fell in love with the bluebonnets she saw from
the airplane window. She quickly fell in love
with Austin, too, and enrolled in the University
of Texas. Lady Bird received a Bachelor of Arts
degree in history with honors in 1933. In 1934
she received a second Bachelor of Arts degree
in journalism cum laude. She was active in
organizations including Texas Orange Jackets.
She also earned a teaching certificate.
— BIRD AND LYNDON got married! —
The couple settled in Washington, DC, after Lyndon
was elected to Congress. After he enlisted
in the navy at the outset of the Second World War,
Lady Bird ran his congressional office.
She used her modest inheritance to bankroll his
congressional campaign. She bought a radio station
and, later, a television station, which made the
Johnsons millionaires.

Johnson was an advocate for beautifying the nation's
cities and highways.

        "Where flowers bloom,

            so does hope."

                    --Lady Bird

The HIGHWAY BEAUTIFICATION ACT was informally
known as "Lady Bird's Bill."

She received the Presidential Medal of Freedom
and the Congressional Gold Medal, the highest
honors bestowed upon a US civilan.

HEART ATTACK
July 2, 1955

Forty-six-year-old Lyndon Johnson had his first heart attack when he was serving as a hard-working Senate Majority Leader.

The news that Lyndon was in Maryland's Bethesda Naval Hospital in critical condition shouldn't have come as a huge surprise. LBJ smoked incessantly, drank loads of six-shooter coffee, ate heavy meals, and had an expanding waistline. He carried 220 pounds on his six-foot-three-inch frame.

He obviously survived, as he became president of the United States eight years later. He did, however, leave the hospital weighing 175 pounds and on a strict diet. The goal was to reduce cholesterol and lose weight. He had to quit smoking cigarettes, doctor's orders. Upon hearing the news of no more smoking, LBJ blurted, "I'd rather have my pecker cut off!"

He did quit smoking and he did keep his weight and waistline down, but there were a number of "doctor's orders" he declined to follow. A few things he was told by his doctor include: Consider gravies, rich sauces as poison. Avoid (sweetened) soft drinks and choose instead a low-calorie liquid such as tea with lemon, black coffee in moderation, or a dietic bottled drink. Avoid alcoholic beverages; there is no nutritional value.

6

LADY Bird

Lady Bird is no doubt the most gracious
lady that ever lived.

On her first date with Lyndon, Lyndon proposed.
They were at the Driskill Hotel having a nice
evening, Lady Bird described it as, "a moth
drawn to a flame" She did not want to rush
into marriage and waited 10 weeks.
The couple married on November 17, 1934, at
St. Mark's Episcopal Church in San Antonio, TX.

THE END

JFK chose LBJ as his running mate for the 1960
election. Since Jackie Kennedy was pregnant,
JFK asked Lady Bird to step up to an expanded
role during the campaign. Over 71 days, Lady
Bird travelled 35,000 miles through 11 states
and appeared at 150 events.   I'm tired!

Within her first year as Second Lady, she had
substituted for Jackie at over 50 events.
This experience prepared Lady Bird for what was
to come. She was probably one of the best-qualified
persons to ever step into the role of First Lady.

She had behind her twenty-seven years of experience
on the national political scene.

She was the partner, confidante, and helpmate
of a man that rose from a job as congressional
secretary to Member of Congress, serving twelve
years in the Senate- six of these as Majority
Leader and then three years as Vice President.

She traveled to thirty-three foreign countries
in less than three years.

She was especially interested in what she calls
the woman-doers of each nation and asked especially
to have a chance to meet these women, to learn
the problems of each country and how they are
trying to solve them.

When Mrs. Johnson became First Lady, the
woman-doers of our own country became her
honored guests at White House luncheons.

"WOMAN-DOERS"
--Lady Bird felt these woman should be
admired.

7

Breakfast

MUESLI

3/4 cup old-fashion rolled oats
6 chopped, sun-dried Black Mission figs
1/4 teaspoon ground cinnamon
2/3 cup water
1/2 medium-sized apple
1 banana, sliced
1 cup plain, low-fat yogurt
8 almonds or hazelnuts, chopped

Combine oats, figs, cinnamon and cover with water and soak overnight.

Before serving, grate apple and stir into oat mixture. Divide into 4 portions, add a few slices of the banana.

Top with 1/4 cup yogurt sprinkled with nuts.

Note: Other sun-dried fruits such as apricots or dates can be used.

Mother's Whole Wheat Pancakes

2/3 cup stone-ground whole wheat flour
1/3 cup all-purpose flour
1/4 cup regular whole wheat flour
2 tsp. wheat germ
2 tsp. brown sugar
1 tsp. baking powder
1/2 tsp. baking soda
pinch salt
1 cup buttermilk
1/4 cup skim milk
1 large egg
1 egg white
1 tsp. vegetable oil
1/2 tsp. vanilla

Combine dry ingredients. Whisk wet ingredients
separately until eggs are light. Combine dry and
wet ingredients, stirring just enough to combine.
Heat griddle to medium high; reduce to medium low
just before ladling on batter. Cook the first side
of cakes until bubbles all pop, then flip and brown
the other side. Serves four.

YOGURT PEACH FRUIT SAUCE FOR MOTHER'S PANCAKES

2 cups plain lowfat yogurt
1/2 teaspoon orange zest
nutmeg to taste
1 tablespoon honey
3 ripe peaches, sliced

Stir zest into yogurt. Sprinkle with nutmeg
and drizzle honey over the top. Place peach
segments in a bowl on the side. Allow each
person about 1/3 cup of the yogurt sauce and
some slices with their pancakes.

H·O·E

Hoecakes

Hoecakes or johnnycakes are traditional pancakes that are popular in the South.

Hoecakes are small pancakes made from cornmeal. The name "hoecake" can also refer to fried cornbread. Hoecakes are crispy on the edges and have a much denser texture than regular ol' pancakes. In other words, expect a thick dough, not pancakey.

Ingredients

C·A·K·E·S

1 1/4 cups flour
1 1/4 cups cornmeal
2 beaten eggs
1 tsp. baking powder
1 tsp. baking soda
1 Tbsp. sugar
1 cup buttermilk (LBJ loved buttermilk)
1/4 cup canola oil
1/4 cup boiling water (important!)

Combine first 8 ingredients in a bowl and mix. Then quickly add boiling water and mix with a wooden spoon.

Heat cast iron pan; add cooking oil and heat until oil is very hot. For each cake, pour a large spoonful of batter into pan. When the bottom of the cake is golden brown, flip and cook the other side until golden. Remove from heat, drain briefly if necessary, and serve hot.

Buttermi

Makes about 15 hoecakes. !!! Ho·Ho·Ho!

2 EGGS

Boiling water

baking powder
baking soda
Sugar

Ranch Pancakes

2 cups flour
1/2 cup sugar
3 teaspoons baking powder
2 cups skim milk
4 oz. butter
1 egg
1 teaspoon vanilla

Whisk dry ingredients together. Blend in skim milk and soft butter. Add egg and stir until all ingredients are blended, but do not over-mix. Place batter by the spoonful on hot griddle. Turn each pancake after bubbles stop forming.

Granola
This is a favorite of Luci's

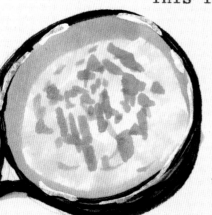

1/2 cup vegetable oil
4 cups rolled oats
1 cup sliced almonds
2 cups whole wheat flakes
1/2 cup sesame seeds
3/4 cup honey
1 teaspoon vanilla

Heat oil in a heavy skillet. Place oats and almonds in the skillet and stir constantly over medium heat for 5 minutes to toast a little. Add whole wheat flakes and sesame seeds. (The sesame seeds are a MUST in this recipe.) Keep stirring and heating for about 10 minutes. Add honey and vanilla and stir for 2 to 3 minutes or more. Store in air-tight container. Do not make more than 3 or 4 days ahead as it does not stay fresh long. 230 calories per cup.

Tiny Quiches

Filling:

1/2 cup homemade bacon bits
1/2 cup grated Monterey jack
    cheese
1 Tbsp. dried parsley
2 eggs, well beaten
paprika

1/2 cup half-and-half
1/2 tsp. salt
dash Tabasco sauce
dash nutmeg
1 Tbsp. grated Parmesan

Crusts:

3 oz. cream cheese
1/2 cup butter
1 cup flour, sifted

Bring butter and cream cheese to room temperature to soften, then blend together. Stir in flour. Chill 1 hour. Shape into 2 dozen one-inch balls. Place in tiny muffin tins, greased lightly or sprayed with cooking spray. Press dough onto bottom and sides of muffin cups. Layer bacon, cheese, and parsley in unbaked crust. Beat together the next 5 ingredients and pour over bacon, cheese, and parsley mix. Sprinkle Parmesan cheese and paprika on top. Bake at 325F for 25 to 35 minutes. (Quiches baked in regular-size muffin tins take 10-15 minutes longer to bake.) Makes 24 mini or 12 larger quiches.

These are made when Lynda Bird and Luci are at the ranch.

14

Buttermilk Biscuits

2 cups flour	3 Tablespoons shortening
6 teaspoons baking powder	1/2 teaspoon baking soda
1 teaspoon salt	1 cup fresh buttermilk

Combine flour, baking powder, and salt. Cut in shortening until consistency is coarse.

Add baking soda to buttermilk; stir into flour mixture. Mix well.

Roll dough on floured board and cut into rounds. Bake at 450F om ungreased baking sheet for 10-12 minutes, or until browned.

Makes 12- 15 large biscuits.

LOVE!

GRITS!!!!!!!

⭐ YA'LL GOTTA KNOW ABOUT GRITS

...CAUSE WE'S ALWAYS FIXIN' EM

If you don't know what grits are. DO NOT admit it. REALLY! (especially to a Texan)

grits

noun, plural in form but singular or plural in construction

⭐ coarsely ground hulled grain; especially : ground hominy with the germ removed

⭐ Origin: perhaps partly from

1 grit, partly from dialect grit course meal, from Old English grytt; akin to the Old English greot.

First known use:: 1579

--from: Merriam-Webster
⭐ Dictionary

Yes I do!

Do you? Love do you? LOVE LOVE GRITS?

TRADITIONAL RECIPE

Add one cup of grits to four cups of boiling water, and add 1 teaspoon salt.

Bring to a boil, reduce heat to medium, cover and cook about 20 or 30 minutes, stirring often to prevent sticking.(Additional water may be added for the desired consistency, as the grits cook). Adding milk makes grits creamy.

Serve hot with lots of butter or with gravy.

Serves 4

1 stick $=$ lotsa Butta

$+$

1 grits. $+$

1   2   3

4

4 cups of water.

Boil Grits

Bran Muffins

1 15-oz box Raisin Bran

1 cup melted shortening or oil

3 cups sugar

4 eggs (beaten)

1 quart buttermilk

5 cups white flour

2 tsp. baking powder

3 tsp. baking soda

2 tsp. salt

Mix dry ingredients in a large bowl.

Mix eggs, oil, and buttermilk together,

then add dry ingredients. Mix well.

Butter or oil a muffin tin and fill
each cup 3/4 full of batter. Bake
15-20 minutes at 375F.

Healthy Refrigerator Bran Muffins ------

2 1/2 cups All-Bran cereal

8 oz. seedless raisins

1 cup sugar

1 cup boiling water

1 cup vegetable oil

4 oz. chopped prunes

1 cup molasses

2 eggs, well-beaten

2 cups buttermilk

2 1/2 cups whole wheat flakes (cereal)

2 1/2 tsp. baking soda

2 tsp. salt

Pre-heat oven to 375F. Combine 1 cup all-bran and raisins in a bowl and pour hot water over it. Set aside.

Mix oil, molasses, eggs, buttermilk and remaining bran in a bowl. Stir well after each addition. Sift flour, salt, and soda together and add to mixture. Stir well. Add this to the cooled bran and raisin mixture. Fill greased muffin tin 2/3 full.

Bake 15 minutes. Cool slightly, enjoy!

19

Popovers

- 1 cup sifted flour
- 1 cup milk
- 2 eggs, beaten
- 1/4 teaspoon salt
- 2 tablespoons shortening (melted)

Mix and sift flour and salt. Combine eggs, milk and shortening; gradually add to flour mixture, beating about one minute or until batter is smooth.

Fill greased sizzling hot pans three-quarters full and bake in very hot oven (450) about 20 minutes--then reduce heat to a moderate (350) oven and continue baking for 15 to 20 minutes.

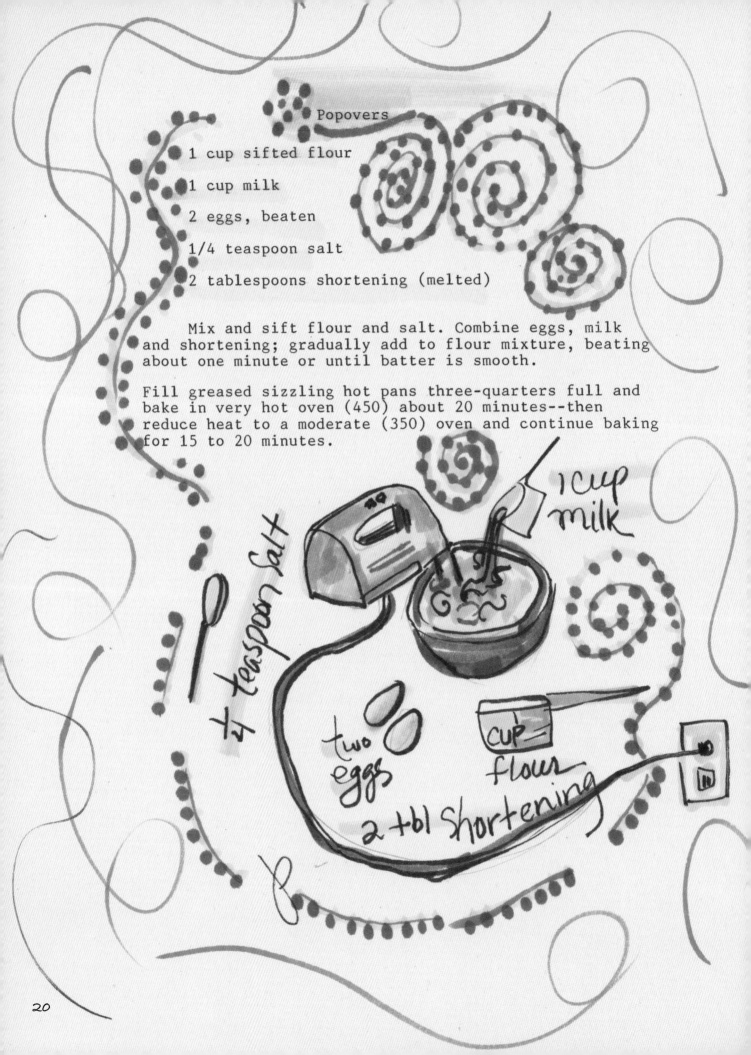

Susan's Sweet Rolls

2 sticks butter
1 cup sugar
1 tsp. salt
1 cup boiling water
2 eggs, beaten
2 pkgs. active dry yeast
1 cup warm water
6 cups white flour

butter
cinnamon sugar
chopped pecans

Pour boiling water over butter to melt. Add sugar and salt; blend together and cool. Sprinkle yeast over warm water and let dissolve. Add beaten eggs to yeast mixture. Combine sugar/salt/water and yeast mixtures before stirring in flour. The mixture will be sticky. Cover with foil and refrigerate for at least 24 hours; remove from refrigerator at least 3 hours before baking. Divide dough into two equal parts. Roll each into a rectangle; spread softened butter, cinnamon sugar, and chopped nuts over dough. Roll up and pinch along seam to seal; slice and let rise for 3 hours. Place on buttered cookie sheets or in buttered muffin tins.

Bake on 425* oven for 10 to 15 minutes. Makes about 50 rolls.

ICING

1/3 cup butter, melted
2 cups powdered sugar
1 1/2 tsp. vanilla
2-4 TBSP. milk

Mix butter, sugar and vanilla. Add milk as needed. Spread over warm rolls with a knife.

Sprinkle with finely chopped pecans.

① Add:
Butta, sugar, vanilla
② mix
③ THEN ADD Just enough milk
④ THEN Stir, ice rolls. enjoy!

Appetizers

Cheese Puffs
recipe from Mollie Parnis - an American
530 Seventh Ave.   Fashion Designer.
New York, NY   Lady Bird liked + bought
her dresses from her NYC
studio.

1 cup water
1 stick of butter
1 teaspoon salt
1/8 teaspoon pepper
Pinch nutmeg
1 tablespoon parmesan cheese
1/4 teaspoon dry mustard
1 cup all purpose flour
   sifted/ measure and sweep off excess
5 eggs

Place water, butter, salt, pepper, cheese,
mustard, and nutmeg in a heavy 2-quart saucepan. Bring to a boil, remove from heat,
and immediately pour in the flour. Stir
with a wooden spoon until dough gathers in
the center and the sides of the pan are
clean. Make a depression in the center
of the dough, break an egg into it, and
beat until egg is incorporated. Repeat,
adding and beating in the rest of the eggs
one by one. Heat 1 inch of oil in a skillet
until very hot. Drop batter in by demitasse-
size spoonsful. Cook until lightly browned;
drain, sprinkle with cheese,
and serve.

grate me please

Cheese Block

CHEESE WAFERS
(FROM OLGA BREDT)

- 1 cup soft butter
- 2 cups flour
- 8 OZ. grated sharp cheddar cheese
- 1 TSP. Cayenne Pepper (perhaps more)
- 1 TSP. Salt
- 2 cups puffed cereal (such as Rice Krispies)

Cut butter into flour, add cheese and seasonings.

Fold in cereal. Drop small rounds onto ungreased cookie sheet and flatten slightly.

Bake in 350F oven for about 15 minutes.

Chili Con Queso

--this is part of the food group found in Texas.
includes, nachos, enchiladas, refried beans aka
re-used beans per the Queen of England.
Most anything on a Tex-Mex menu is included
in a food group known to Texans only.

- Queso------- for short. Queso is chili con queso
- 1 10-ounce can of Ro-Tel
- 1 pound American Cheese aka Velveeta aka plastic cheese

- Warm restaurant style tortilla chips

- Cut Velveeta into cubes and mix with Rotel in a
microwave-safe bowl. Microwave on high for about
one minute; stir and heat again. Continue heating
and stirring until mixture
is smooth and creamy.
Serve hot with chips.

- The Johnsons were friendly and gregarious and
they enveloped the White House in a warm, convivial
atmosphere. Even the State Dinners and other formal
functions seemed relaxed, enjoyable.
The aura of the White House had been transformed by
this Texan family from French to informal Western
American.

- The rule is-----if you can't stand Texas cooking,
get out of the kitchen!!!

- And that is what the French Chef hired by Jackie--O
did.

adios amigo!

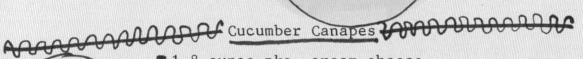

Cucumber Canapes

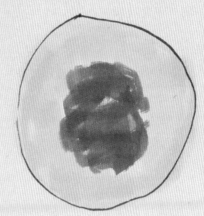

- 1 8-ounce pkg. cream cheese
- 1 cucumber
- 2 celery sticks
- 1 green pepper
- 2 stuffed olives
- 1 green onion
- mayo
- white bread
- butter

Soften cream cheese and mix with mayo.
Sprinkle with salt and pepper.
Finely chop other ingredients and mix
with cream cheese.
Cut bread into 1½" circles (four to a slice).
First spread bread with thin layer of butter.
Then spread layer of cream cheese mixture.

CHUTNEY STUFFED EGGS

- 12 hard-boiled eggs
- ½ cup finely chopped chutney
- 6 slices of bacon
- 3 tablespoons mayo

B.A.C.O.N

Cut eggs in half. Remove yolks and mash. Cook
and crumble bacon and add to mashed yolks
together with chutney and mayo. Fill egg white
with mixture; use a pastry tube for a pretty
effect. Makes 24 crunchy, sweet hors d'oeuvres.

+ EGGS

deviled eggs

Deviled Eggs

8 hard-cooked eggs

1/2 cup mayonnaise

2 teaspoons heavy cream

2 teaspoons vinegar

2 teaspoons prepared mustard

1/2 teaspoon sugar

1/2 teaspoon salt

1/8 teaspoon pepper

Cut eggs into halves lengthwise and then into quarters: remove yolks. Press egg yolks through a fine sieve; blend in remaining ingredients. Spoon mixture into a cake-decorating bag with a star tip and stuff cooked egg whites.

Serves 8 to 12.

"KISSIN' DON'T LAST, COOKIN' DO"

what's Cookin? good Lookin

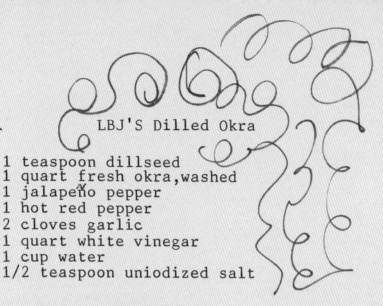

LBJ'S Dilled Okra

1 teaspoon dillseed
1 quart fresh okra,washed
1 jalapeño pepper
1 hot red pepper
2 cloves garlic
1 quart white vinegar
1 cup water
1/2 teaspoon uniodized salt

Place 1/2 teaspoon dillseed in bottom of a
2-quart sterilized jar.
Pack okra as tightly as possible in the jar,
without bruising. Sprinkle remainder of the
dillseed over the top, and press peppers
and garlic among the okra.
Bring vinegar, water, and salt to a boil and
pour over the okra.
Seal jars and allow to stand 2 weeks.
Before serving, chill in refrigerator.

Makes about 2 quarts.

MARINATED SHRIMP

1 cup vinegar
1 tablespoon hot mustard
   (prepared)
1 clove garlic
   (crushed)
1/8 teaspoon salt
2 pounds cooked
  shrimp, deveined
  and chilled.

1 cup olive oil

1/2 cup chopped scallions

1/2 cup chili sauce
2 tablespoons paprika

Bibb lettuce

Crisp toast points

Mix vinegar, olive oil, mustard, scallions, garlic, chili
sauce, salt, and paprika together; pour over shrimp
in a large bowl and marinate at least 8 hours or overnight.

Turn shrimp several times during marinating. Drain
and serve on bed of lettuce with toast points. Serves
10 to 12.

CUBED ROAST BEEF WITH HORSE-RADISH WHIPPED
CREAM DIP

1 cup chilled heavy cream
Cold roast beef cut in cubes

1/4 cup prepared horse-
   radish

Whip cream until stiff; fold in horseradish. Chill
about 1/2 hour before serving. At serving time place
dip in a bowl in center of a large platter and surround
with cubes of cold roast beef on toothpicks.
Makes about two cups.

COCKTAIL SPARERIBS

5 lbs. pork spareribs
1 cup soy sauce
1/2 teaspoon garlic powder

1 cup orange marmalade
1 chopped, medium sized onion
1/2 teaspoon ground black pepper

Have butcher cut flat bone end of each sparerib section
into two 2-inch strips across the bones. Put ribs in a
large, deep bowl. Heat orange marmalade and soy sauce
until marmalade is melted; remove from heat and add onion
garlic powder and pepper. Pour over ribs and marinate in
refrigerator for 12 hours or overnight, turning to coat ribs.
Heat oven to 325F. Arrange ribs on rack in large roasting
pan and baste with sauce. Bake uncovered 1 1/2 hours,
basting occasionally with the sauce, until golden brown.
Turn once while baking. Serve hot. Serves 8

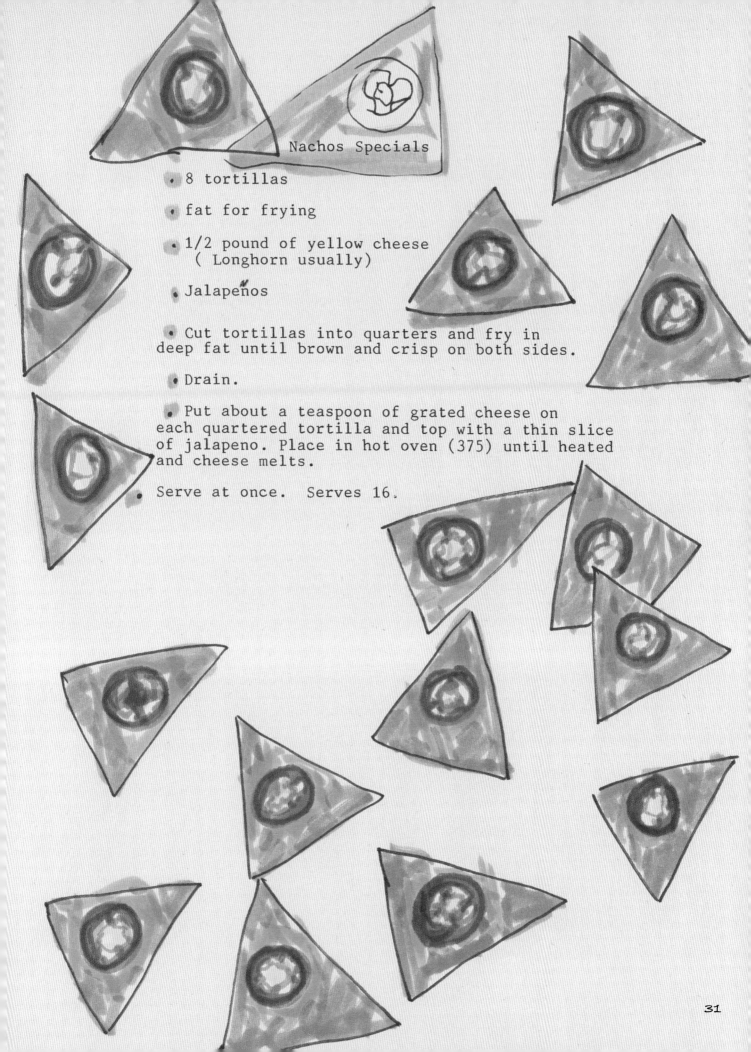

Nachos Specials

- 8 tortillas

- fat for frying

- 1/2 pound of yellow cheese
  (Longhorn usually)

- Jalapeños

- Cut tortillas into quarters and fry in deep fat until brown and crisp on both sides.

- Drain.

- Put about a teaspoon of grated cheese on each quartered tortilla and top with a thin slice of jalapeno. Place in hot oven (375) until heated and cheese melts.

Serve at once. Serves 16.

31

PATE

Mrs. J says, "Good for parties". . . and
"This pate will feed 25-28 people well."

1 pkg. unflavored gelatin
1 can beef consomme (10 or 12 oz.)
1/2 cup liverwurst
6 oz. cream cheese
2 Tbsp. whipping cream
2 Tbsp. sherry
1/2 tsp. Beau Monde seasoning
Squeeze of garlic
Shake of Tabasco sauce
Shake of red pepper
Dissolve gelatin in hot consomme; cool
mixture slightly. Place in blender with
remaining ingredients and blend well.
Pour into mold and chill thoroughly.
Serve with crackers.

famous

PICADILLO MEAT DIP

1 lb. ground beef
1 onion, chopped
1 cup chopped tomatoes,
    fresh or canned
2 garlic cloves, pressed
1 Tbsp. vinegar
¼ tsp. ground cumin
1 tsp. salt

1 bay leaf
1/2 tsp. oregano, or
    1 tsp. cinnamon and
    a pinch of cloves
2 whole jalapeños, chopped
1/2 cup raisins
1/2 cup slivered almonds

Place meat in frying pan along with the onion
and garlic. When the meat has browned, add all
but the raisins and almonds and simmer for 30
minutes. Next add raisins and almonds, simmer for
5 to 10 minutes. This can be used for taco filling
or serve warm with scrambled eggs. If used as a
dip you can thin with tomato juice. Freeze and
use later if desired. Serves 6 to 8.

RAW VEGETABLE BOWL AND DIP

1 8-ounce package cream cheese, at room temp.
1 cup sour cream (not fat-free)
2 teaspoons grated white onion
1 clove garlic, mashed
2 teaspoons Worcestershire sauce
1 teaspoon dry mustard
2 teaspoons anchovy paste (optional)
cherry tomatoes thinly sliced
zucchini, cauliflowerettes, carrot
strips, celery strips, pickled
okra.

Beat together cream cheese and sour cream;
and onion, garlic, Worcestershire and
mustard. If desired blend in anchovy
paste.

Chill at least one hour. Pour into small
bowl in center of large plate and surround
with vegetables.

Celery

vegetable thin sticks

chopped carrot

Cauliflowerettes

thinly sliced zucchini

P·A·R·S·L·E·Y

Spinach Spread

Spinach Spread.

1 pkg. frozen spinach, (chopped)
thaw, drain and squeeze excess water
until dry.

1/2 cup chopped parsley

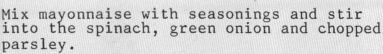
1/2 cup chopped green onion with tops

1 cup mayonnaise
1 tablespoon salad seasoning
(Herbes de Provence)
1 tablespoon dill weed

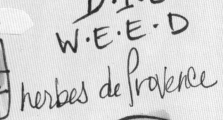

D·I·L·L
W·E·E·D
herbes de Provence

MAYO

Mix mayonnaise with seasonings and stir
into the spinach, green onion and chopped
parsley.
As you begin to double and triple this
recipe, do not use as much mayo. I (Lady Bird)
use 1 1/2 cup for double, a little over 2 cups
for 3, etc. But do use the listed proportions
of everything else. This is better if made the
day before so the spices get to know each
other. Will keep in fridge for days.

Green onion

Party Clam Dip........

2 large (8 oz.) pkgs. cream cheese, very soft
2 cans minced clams; drain all but 1 tsp. juice
3 tsp. lemon juice
1 tsp. red pepper
2 Tbsp. onion juice
1 tsp. Tabasco sauce
1 clove garlic, pressed, or equivalent in onion powder
½ cup real mayonnaise

Mix ingredients by hand. Heat in chafing dish. Do not
overheat, or ingredients will separate. Serve with melba
rounds or plain crackers. Best if made the day before.

Stuffed Mushrooms

2 dozen small mushrooms or 6 large

Olive oil   4 tablespoons butter

1 onion, finely minced   1 stalk celery finely
                                          minced

1 clove garlic, finely minced

1 tablespoon dried parsley flakes

1/2 teaspoon salt   Dash cayenne pepper

3 slices bread, made into crumbs in the blender

Parmesan cheese

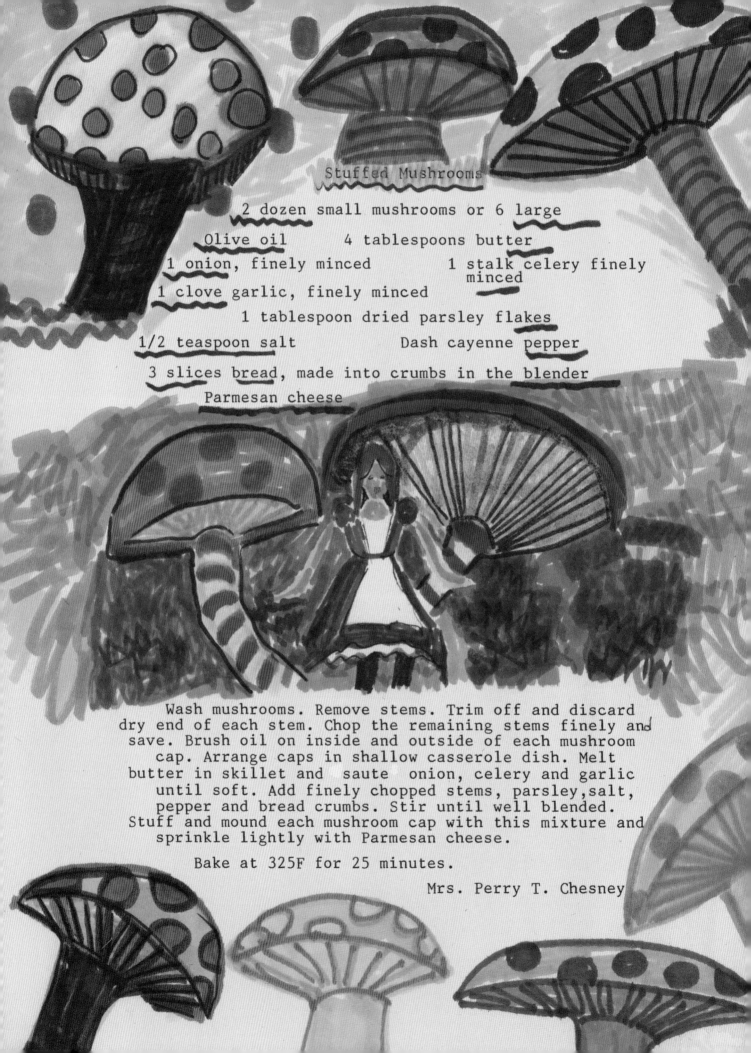

Wash mushrooms. Remove stems. Trim off and discard
dry end of each stem. Chop the remaining stems finely and
save. Brush oil on inside and outside of each mushroom
cap. Arrange caps in shallow casserole dish. Melt
butter in skillet and saute onion, celery and garlic
until soft. Add finely chopped stems, parsley, salt,
pepper and bread crumbs. Stir until well blended.
Stuff and mound each mushroom cap with this mixture and
sprinkle lightly with Parmesan cheese.

Bake at 325F for 25 minutes.

Mrs. Perry T. Chesney

DON'T MESS WITH TEXAS!

━━ TeXaS TrAsH ━━

(From Sudie Campbell, Marg's mom)

You Know... Marg!

1 box Cheerios
1 box Rice Chex (or any flavor Chex)
1 box tiny pretzel sticks
1 Tbsp. garlic salt
1 Tbsp. savory salt
1 Tbsp. Tabasco sauce
1 Tbsp. Worcestershire Sauce
1 stick butter or margarine
1 lb. pecans or mixed nuts (Lady Bird used
more than 1 lb.)

Mix Cheerios, Chex, and pretzels together.
Add nuts and mix again. Melt butter or
margarine; add seasonings and mix.

In a large, flat pan (Lady Bird used a
turkey roaster), add cereal mixture and
pour seasoned, melted butter or margarine
over it. Mix well.

Heat uncovered in 350F oven for 20-25
minutes, stirring often.

At the Ranch

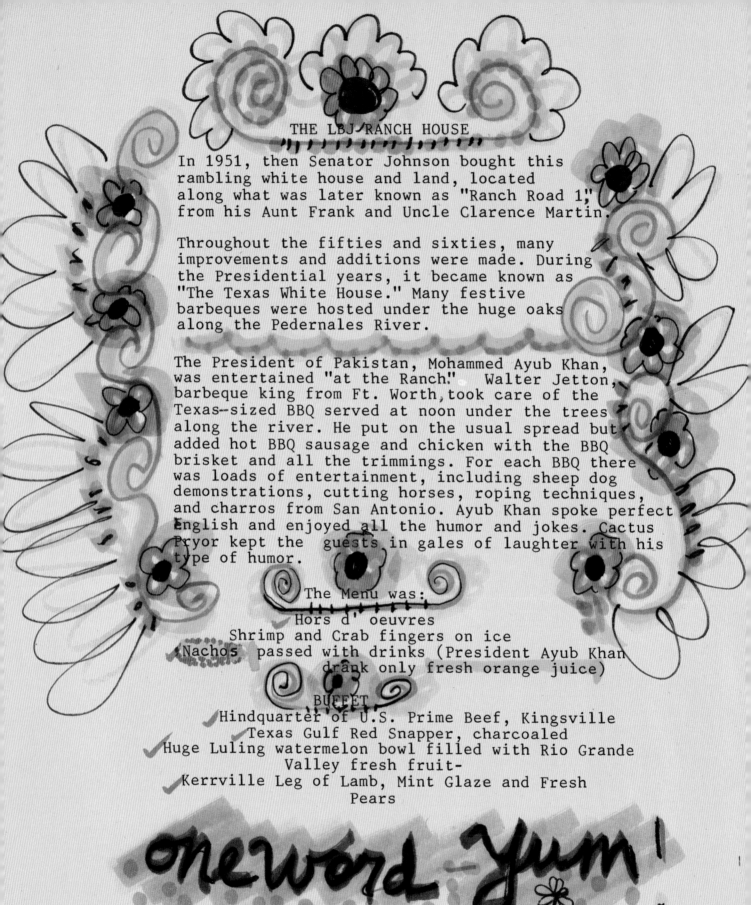

THE LBJ RANCH HOUSE

In 1951, then Senator Johnson bought this
rambling white house and land, located
along what was later known as "Ranch Road 1,"
from his Aunt Frank and Uncle Clarence Martin.

Throughout the fifties and sixties, many
improvements and additions were made. During
the Presidential years, it became known as
"The Texas White House." Many festive
barbeques were hosted under the huge oaks
along the Pedernales River.

The President of Pakistan, Mohammed Ayub Khan,
was entertained "at the Ranch!" Walter Jetton,
barbeque king from Ft. Worth, took care of the
Texas-sized BBQ served at noon under the trees
along the river. He put on the usual spread but
added hot BBQ sausage and chicken with the BBQ
brisket and all the trimmings. For each BBQ there
was loads of entertainment, including sheep dog
demonstrations, cutting horses, roping techniques,
and charros from San Antonio. Ayub Khan spoke perfect
English and enjoyed all the humor and jokes. Cactus
Pryor kept the guests in gales of laughter with his
type of humor.

The Menu was:

Hors d' oeuvres
Shrimp and Crab fingers on ice
Nachos passed with drinks (President Ayub Khan
drank only fresh orange juice)

BUFFET

Hindquarter of U.S. Prime Beef, Kingsville
Texas Gulf Red Snapper, charcoaled
Huge Luling watermelon bowl filled with Rio Grande
Valley fresh fruit-
Kerrville Leg of Lamb, Mint Glaze and Fresh
Pears

one word - yum!

LBJ LOVED HIS VEHICLES

He loved his Lincoln Continental Convertibles.
I saw Lbj and Lady Bird in a Lincoln when I was 11 years old.

this is like the → car @ the museum *in austin.*

The people of Brady, Texas gave LBJ a 1915 Fire Truck

The fun car was his Amphicar. LBJ surprised guests when taking them for a ride around the ranch in an Amphicar.

ah.. Help!

Imagine you are near the Pedernales River in the amphicar, when LBJ yells, "The brakes don't work, No brakes! (you are going down hill at this point headed straight for the river). LBJ continues yelling, No brakes, we are going in! Hold on! You are about to jump when the car levels off and is now floating like a boat. LBJ laughs; you realize he knew the whole time what was going on. Well, that experience would be a typical ride in LBJ's Amphicar.

very cool car ←

The Jolly 500 Ghia
A rare auto and a gift from the Fiat Company.

Cushman Gold Carts- used to transport important people around the ranch, to and fro from the airstrip.

The president was given a DONKEY CART. He would hitch up his two donkeys, Soup and Noodles, and give kids a ride around the property.

Soup *Noodles*

"One of my favorite times of the year is the Hill Country
in Spring, slipping into early summer, while it's still
pleasantly cool outside.
Guests frequently arrive mid-afternoon and are greeted
with tall glasses of iced spiced tea with sprigs of mint
from our garden, and plates of sand tarts and lace cookies.
The tea, served under the large live oak trees, is
delicious (or equally good served hot in our best cups on
a chilly winter afternoon in front of the fireplace)."

— Lady Bird

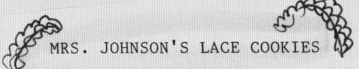

MRS. JOHNSON'S LACE COOKIES

1/2 cup flour	1/4 cup brown sugar, firmly packed
1/2 cup coconut	1/4 cup KARO syrup (red or blue label)
1/4 cup butter	1/2 teaspoon salt

Mix flour with coconut. Cook butter, Karo
syrup, sugar, and salt over medium heat,
stirring constantly, until sugar is
completely dissolved. Remove from heat, stir
in vanilla, then gradually blend in flour
mixture. Drop by teaspoons 3 inches apart on
an ungreased cookie sheet. Bake at 325F for 8
to 10 minutes, or until lightly browned.

Cool one minute, remove from cookie sheet,
and finish cooling on a wire rack. Makes 4 to
5 dozen 2" cookies.

...for sand tarts, see Desserts.

Mrs. Johnson was quite the hostess at the ranch and the White House.

When Lady Bird had guests at the ranch, she had beautiful flower arrangements in all the rooms. She also had fresh fruits and Lammes candies in each room, and every morning room service delivered coffee in a thermos pitcher. A country breakfast was served in the dining room. She often served popovers and venison sausage.

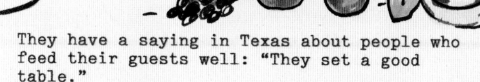

They have a saying in Texas about people who feed their guests well: "They set a good table."

Well, no surprise President and Mrs. Johnson set a good table. Lean bacon and prime beef from their ranch animals...catfish and bass from their ponds and rivers...vegetables from their garden...fresh peaches, homemade preserves and jellies were served to their guests.

The dining room at the ranch is modest in size, seats about twelve comfortably. Mr. Johnson sits at one end of the table in an office swivel chair; Lady Bird at the other end, with her foot near a buzzer to summon a waiter to bring more rolls, etc.

Precautions were taken with Mr. Johnson's diet. Placed in front of him was a bottle of artificial no-calorie sweetener. He had been known to cheat, however. On one occasion, Lady Bird was called to the telephone, and upon her departure Mr. Johnson reached over, got a large saucer of jelly, and ate it all with a teaspoon.

Q. Tell what it was like to work for LBJ?

A. That would take about six hours.

It was sort of a challenge to keep up with what he expected of you. He, also, expected perfection. I don't think either one of them had much tolerance for mistakes, for errors, which is good. It might be to the point of being--I know he has been accused of being a slave driver and so forth. I've never felt that way.

But he's a perfectionist himself;

she is too; and they ex-

pect it of their staff. They expect

them to put as much time into

things as they do.

Each letter that we wrote, we thought, "That may

be the only letter this person

will ever get from the President or the

First Lady, and it may go up on the wall,

to be the very best letter."

— employee

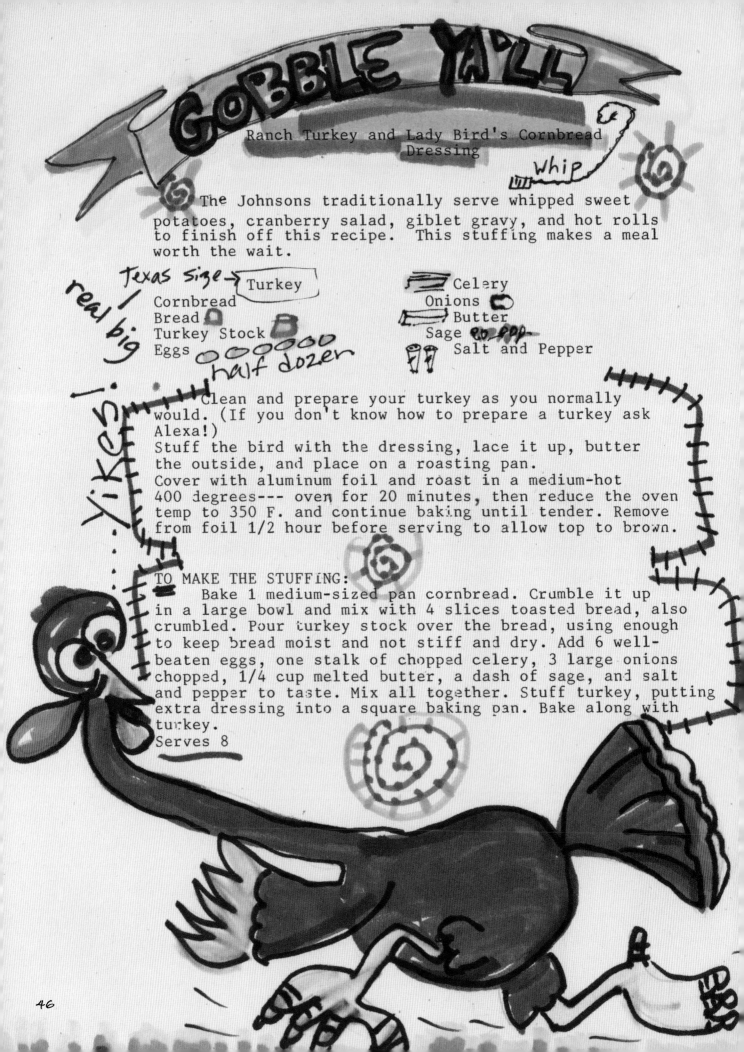

GOBBLE YA'LL

Ranch Turkey and Lady Bird's Cornbread Dressing

Whip

The Johnsons traditionally serve whipped sweet potatoes, cranberry salad, giblet gravy, and hot rolls to finish off this recipe. This stuffing makes a meal worth the wait.

Texas size →
real big!

Turkey	Celery
Cornbread	Onions
Bread	Butter
Turkey Stock	Sage
Eggs *half dozen*	Salt and Pepper

Yikes!

Clean and prepare your turkey as you normally would. (If you don't know how to prepare a turkey ask Alexa!)
Stuff the bird with the dressing, lace it up, butter the outside, and place on a roasting pan.
Cover with aluminum foil and roast in a medium-hot 400 degrees--- oven for 20 minutes, then reduce the oven temp to 350 F. and continue baking until tender. Remove from foil 1/2 hour before serving to allow top to brown.

TO MAKE THE STUFFING:
Bake 1 medium-sized pan cornbread. Crumble it up in a large bowl and mix with 4 slices toasted bread, also crumbled. Pour turkey stock over the bread, using enough to keep bread moist and not stiff and dry. Add 6 well-beaten eggs, one stalk of chopped celery, 3 large onions chopped, 1/4 cup melted butter, a dash of sage, and salt and pepper to taste. Mix all together. Stuff turkey, putting extra dressing into a square baking pan. Bake along with turkey.
Serves 8

Lady Bird reminisced about Christmas at the ranch:

"At the ranch . . . Lyndon would just love going
around on Christmas morning delivering Christmas
presents. He wasn't about to let the US mail do it
for him or a secretary or anything else. He just
loved to load up the car. And his favorite gifts
were a box of candy and a bottle of bourbon or
scotch, or whatever he knew to be, or thought to
be, the favorite drink of the person.

"There were two houses across the river, one of
which is now in the LBJ State Park; people were
still living in it at that time, an elderly couple.
And he would go over and take his liquor and his
candy, and they'd talk about old times and Lyndon's
father and mother, mostly of his father, because
his father was much more attached to the
surrounding area and much more neighborly with
them. And there was always Aunt Kitty, and Aunt
Frank, Melvin Winters, and, of course, the A. W.
Moursunds. The latter two were very much a part of
our lives for years and years."

Lyndon's last Christmas, in 1972: "Lyndon rode
around on a riding lawn mower dressed in a Santa
suit. The mower had a cab on the back of it and it
was loaded with Christmas presents. He was . . .
driving the mower in his Santa suit delivering them
to the children of the folks who worked on our
place and the surrounding places. And then it was
followed by a movie." Lady Bird went on to talk
about the "moving picture machine" that was used,
and that it was nicknamed the "Johnson Bijou."

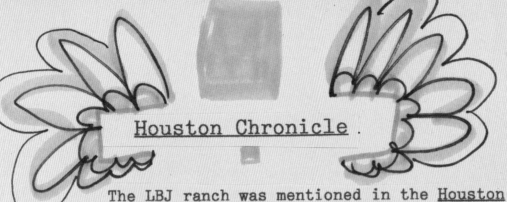

Houston Chronicle.

corn pudding

The LBJ ranch was mentioned in the <u>Houston Chronicle</u> on November 15, 1963, as being famous for its corn pudding, fried catfish, Pedernales chili, venison sausage, golden fried chicken, and pecan pie.

fried catfish

--Appointment file (Diary Back-up)

chili

deer sausage

fried chicken

pecan pie.

Barbecue

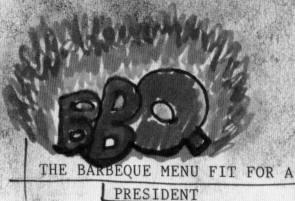

THE BARBEQUE MENU FIT FOR A
PRESIDENT

TEXAS BEEF BARBECUE WITH NATURAL
GRAVY

SMOKED RANCH BEANS

COOKED COUNTRY CORN

COUNTRY POTATO SALAD

TEXAS COLE SLAW

SLICED DILL PICKLE
SPEARS

SPANISH SWEET ONIONS

MODERN DAY SOURDOUGH BISCUITS

FRIED APPLE PIES

SIX-SHOOTER COFFEE

SOFT DRINKS

Legend says that in the early days, a cattle owner,
a Mr. Bernarby Quinn, used a branding iron with his
initials B.Q., with a straight line under the B
Like this: B_Q

He also served the best steaks for 500 miles around.
Thus, Bar-B-Q is synonymous with excellent cook-out
food.

The food for most of LBJ's barbecues was prepared by <u>Walter Jetton</u> (pronounced ji-TON). Jetton ran a popular catering company out of Ft. Worth, Texas, just a few hours from the LBJ ranch.

Jetton was a natural showman. He was usually dressed in a Stetson (hat), apron, white shirt all wrinkled, and a string tie. He billed himself as the "Barbeque King."

Johnson was the first President to hold a barbeque at the White House.
A giant pit was dug in the lawn, and ribs were charbroiled over the fire. The sauce was served on the side, so guests could dip the ribs in it if they wished. The "barbeque king" Walter Jetton prepared all the food for this festive occasion.

BBQ King Walter

Parties were held on Johnson's 2,718-acre ranch and were used as a diplomatic tool to bring people together. He sometimes gave visitors a tour of the ranch by driving 90 miles an hour around the property.

It was Johnson's chief of staff that said, "Politics and baRBEQUE JUST WENT TOGETHER IN TEXAS, WHY not Washington?

ya boss, why not?

guy to know

<u>Chuck-wagon cookin'</u>

by Walter Jetton

"All the folks who come here to eat our chuck seem to like it. Why, when Ludwig Erhard, Chancellor of Germany, came to share our humble fare with us, he ate his steak and pinto beans with just as much enthusiasm as he does frankfurters and sauer- kraut.
"President Johnson likes to eat almost everything. But since he has been President, he's been watching his figure. His favorites of all are barbecued pork spareribs, German-style cole slaw, good steaks, a selection of Spanish pickles, followed by a big tin cup of six-shooter coffee.

"On the LBJ Ranch, called the little White House, we usually entertain people under the live oak trees in the pastureland by the Pedernales River. We give them an old-fashin' chuck-wagon dinner-- plenty of good beef cooked outside over glowing coals, baskets of sour dough biscuits, gallons of sage-scented honey, fresh butter, big red clay pots filled with pinto beans, and bowls of cole slaw."

river

MUST READ

BEEF moo moo

Where to purchase great quality meat.

If you are serious about the art of BBQ, taking off a great piece of meat after alot of work and sweating over the hot grill, then I have some must-read tips for you.

I didn't know the difference in meat either until I did some self-educating and quality meat is not always available at the grocery store.

The best two books about meat are:

1. Lobel's Meat Bible: All you need to know about Meat and Poultry from America's Master Butcher. Author: Stanley Lobel.

2. The Butcher's Apprentice: The Expert's Guide to Selecting, Preparing, and Cooking a World of Meat. Author: Aliza Green

BRISKET TIPS!

Use boneless brisket only. If you have a butcher that knows something about CAB (Certified Angus Brisket) have him/her select a nice piece.

PROPER Texas-style brisket is made with the "packer" cut from a cow. Many grocery stores only sell the "flat" cut, which has the fatty point cut off the meat. You really want the fat!

Sources for meat shipped to you in the US of A

1. Creekstone farms. 1-866-273-3578.

I read that Aaron Franklin gets his brisket here. If you have heard of Franklin's BBQ in Austin, TX then you know what I'm talking about. If you have NOT heards of Franklin's BBQ let me just say that they have sold out of brisket and most of their food every day since they opened. Aaron is famous yo! He has a beautiful BBQ book out with tips! Check it out. Again, Aaron gets his premium black angus, hormone-free, antibiotic-free brisket here. If you watch his tutorials on YouTube you will see that he wraps his beef in 18" pink butcher paper from ABCO in Austin. It's plain paper with no coating of any kind. Therefore the grease soaks through it. I think the beef $$$ may be worth it. This beef has contributed to the success of Franklin's. Aaron won the James Beard Award and his meat was named best BBQ in the USA by Condé Nast in 2010. Bon Appetit said he had the best BBQ in the world. Enough said! OK, one more thing: ABCO Paper— (800)-556-2677

worth the read!

IMPORTANT! READin!

NO to Hormone

No PROMISE. I read it though!

nuff!

52

← order meat to BBQ.

2.) Newell Farmers Market- 1704 Rocky River RD.
    Charlotte, N.C. phone 704-578-1415
    This is a small market but excellent.

3.) Snake River Farms / American Wagyu & Kurobuto
                                    Pork
    snakeriverfarms.com 855-990-3650

4.) LOBELS- A real butcher shop in NYC.
    They sell a natural Prime Beef Brisket that
    is one of their "favorite cuts". If you are
    feeling confused at this point you can order
    their "Whole seasoned beef brisket, 8 lbs."
    It comes with cooking instructions!

5.) Strube Ranch Gourmet Meats
    located in Pittsburg, TX. 903-629-3605
    "The only Wagyu Kosher beef in the industry"

6.) Meyer Natural Foods
    located in Loveland, CO. 888-990-2333
    Vegetarian raised cattle/ no hormones
    or antibiotics

7.) Allen Brothers
    located in Chicago
    Phone orders- 1800-957-0111 /order 24 hours a
                                day/ 7 days a week

8.) Grass & Bone
    located in Mystic, Conn. /butcher shop 860-245-
                                              4814

9.) Belcampo, California
    a leader in the humanely raised animal movement
    --corporate headquarters 510-250-7810

10.) Salt and Time, Austin, TX/fresh cut meats from
     sustainable Texas ranches 512 524-1383

11.) Chicago Steak Company
     888-970-1118

12.) Kansas City Steak Company
     800-987-8325

All the meat resources listed have a website. Google!

Buy the best meat

Buy the best it cooks the best!

meat

②

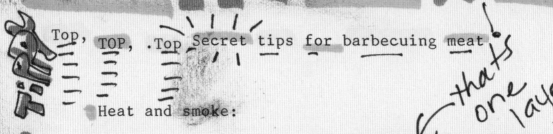

Top, TOP, .Top Secret tips for barbecuing meat

that's one layer

Heat and smoke:

Use one layer of charcoal. *that's one layer*

The heat is going to be pretty low on a BBQ grill, around 220, that is a good heat for most meats!

For SMOKE **220!**

Use a small log placed near the edge of the charcoal. You do not want it to flame up!!!

← log

Charcoal

Whisk Broom

DRIPPING AND FLAMING:

Fat should drip out of the meat slowly, fall on the charcoals and add to the smoke. However, you DO NOT want flaming, that ONLY burns the food. To prevent flaming, keep a whisk broom handy in a can of water. If you get a flame shake a broom of water on it. A water pistol will also work.

STEAM: Shaking water on the coals will give you steam and you should do it every now and then whether you have flaming or not. The steam will hit the meat at a temp. of about 400 to 500 and help you cook it tender.

Don't overdo; 3 or 4 times is enough.

Put on readers

READ THIS CAREFULLY

MOP FOR ALL BARBEQUE MEATS

Put this sauce on a little dish mop and rub it over meats and baste meats while they are cooking. As you use it, the flavor will change and improve. Keep in the refrigerator.

- 3 tablespoons salt
- 3 tablespoons dry mustard
- 2 tablespoons garlic powder
- 1 tablespoon ground bay leaf
- 2 tablespoons chili powder
- 3 tablespoons paprika
- 2 tablespoons hot sauce
- 2 pints Worcestershire sauce
- 1 pint vinegar
- 4 quarts bone stock (beef)
- 1 pint canola or olive oil

MAKES 1½ GALLONS!

Make the bone stock from good stout beef bones bought from a butcher.
Add all the ingredients and cooled bone stock, stir let sit overnight before using.

chili powder

SALT

DRY MUSTARD

Bone stock

GARLIC

Vinegar

SALT

BAY LEAF

MOP SAUCE

FRENCH MARINADE
(For beef, lamb, seafood, veal)

1/2 cup olive oil
1/2 cup wine vinegar
1/4 teaspoon salt
1 clove garlic, crushed
1/8 teaspoon freshly ground pepper
1 tablespoon finely chopped chives

Combine in a jar and shake well

SHAKE
...it Baby shake it!

NOTE: Marinades are pre-cooking sauces and have
two functions:

ONE: TO tenderize meat.

TWO: Give it flavor.

Cover the meat in marinade and let stand
at room temperature for at least an hour
or twelve hours under refrigeration.
The meat should be turned several times.

let stand
ONE
HOUR!

LET STAND ROOM TEMP one hour

James Davis Seasoning for Meats

--This is especially good on Prime Rib and is used often at the Texas White House. James Davis was a long-time employee of the Johnson family serving in many capacities.

1 cup salt

1 cup pepper   1/3 cup onion powder

1/3 cup Accent   1/3 cup garlic powder

Mix all ingredients and rub into the meat before cooking.

Makes about 3 cups.

DRY RUB SEASONING

Sprinkle on spareribs before throwing
on the grill. Do <u>not</u> skimp when applying.

- 6 tablespoons salt
- 6 tablespoons sugar
- 1 tablespoon dry lemon powder
- 2 1/2 tablespoons black pepper
- 1 1/2 tablespoons paprika

**mix it all in bowl.
Apply to ribs.**

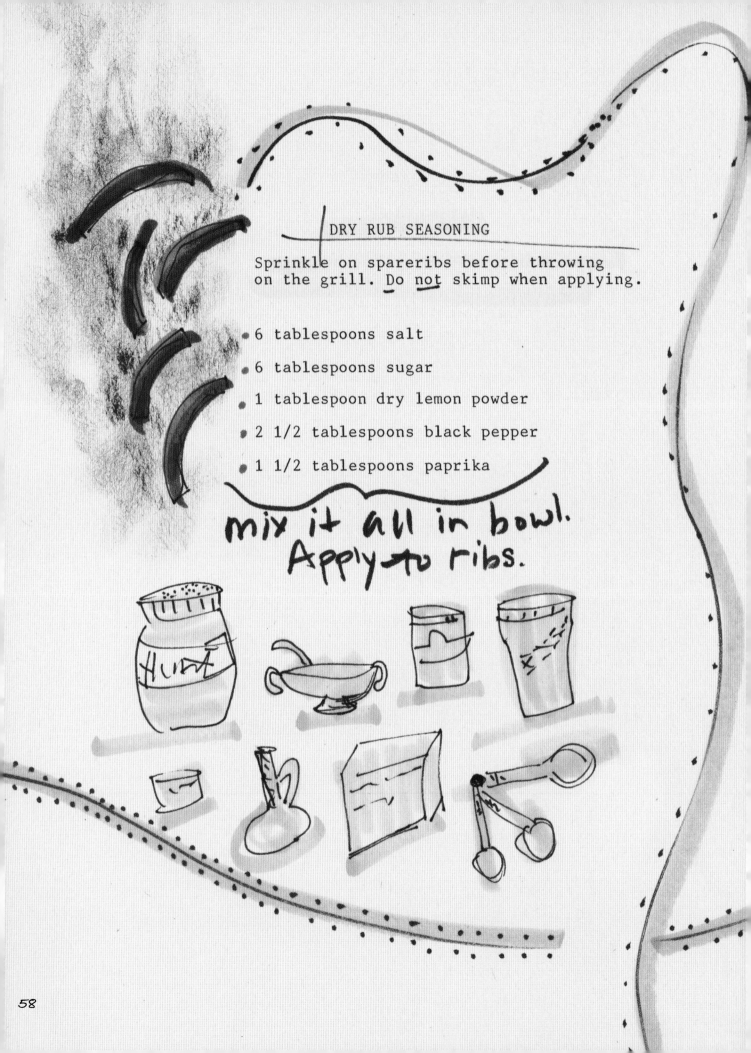

shh! secret shh! shh!

aww!

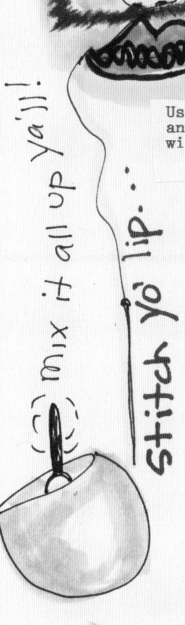

mix it all up ya'll! :-)

stitch yo' lip...

The (secret) BBQ Sauce
The sauce of the ages, guarded
for many years..... now yours!

Use this sauce on beef, chicken, pork, almost
anything. But use it at the table--don't cook
with it.

- 1 cup tomato ketchup
- 1/2 cup cider vinegar
- 1 teaspoon sugar
- 1 teaspoon chili powder
- 1/8 teaspoon salt
- 1 1/2 cups water
- 3 stalks celery, chopped
- 3 bay leaves
- 1 clove garlic
- 2 tablespoons chopped onion
- 4 tablespoons butter
- 4 tablespoons Worcestershire sauce
- 1 teaspoon paprika
- Dash of freshly ground black pepper

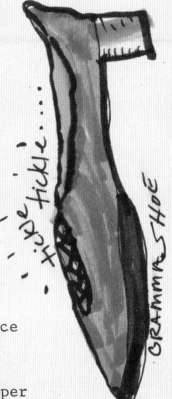

tickle tickle.....

GRAMMA SHOE

Combine all the ingredients and bring to a boil.
Simmer about 15 minutes. Remove from heat and strain.

Makes about 2 1/2 cups

This secret sauce, "would tickle the tongue of
your Grandma's shoe."

At least that is what Walter Jetton~said.

Walter Jetton died at the age of 61 of a heart attack in Ft.
Worth, TX. He was the Barbecue King of all Kings.

SHOE KING

59

TEXAS BEEF BRISKET
BBQ

- 6 pounds beef brisket
- 2 quarts bone stock
- 3 bay leaves
- salt and pepper

Put the bay leaves in about a cup of water and bring to a boil. Let it simmer 10 minutes or so, then remove the leaves and add the bay tea to the bone stock, along with the salt and pepper. Put the brisket in a dutch oven and add the stock mixture to cover it about a quarter of the way. Cover and cook over the fire, turning about every half hour until it's nearly done. This can be done by placing a fork into the meat. Mop it and place it on a hot grill to finish cooking. Be sure to turn and mop every 20 minutes or so. To make a good natural gravy, add alittle Worcest- ershire sauce and a dash of chili powder to the liquid you cooked the brisket in.

BIG DEAL!

Ready carefully!

CAT SUP

Notes from the BBQ boss, Walter Jetton.

1. Do not use ketchup in any form until you are through cooking.

2. BBQ has to be cooked with wood or wood coals at about 275

3. Do not have a big fire under the meat. If a fire should start from grease of the meat, put it out with a cup of water.

4. Cook with coals only.

Bay leaves

COALS ONLY

AGUA

WOOD

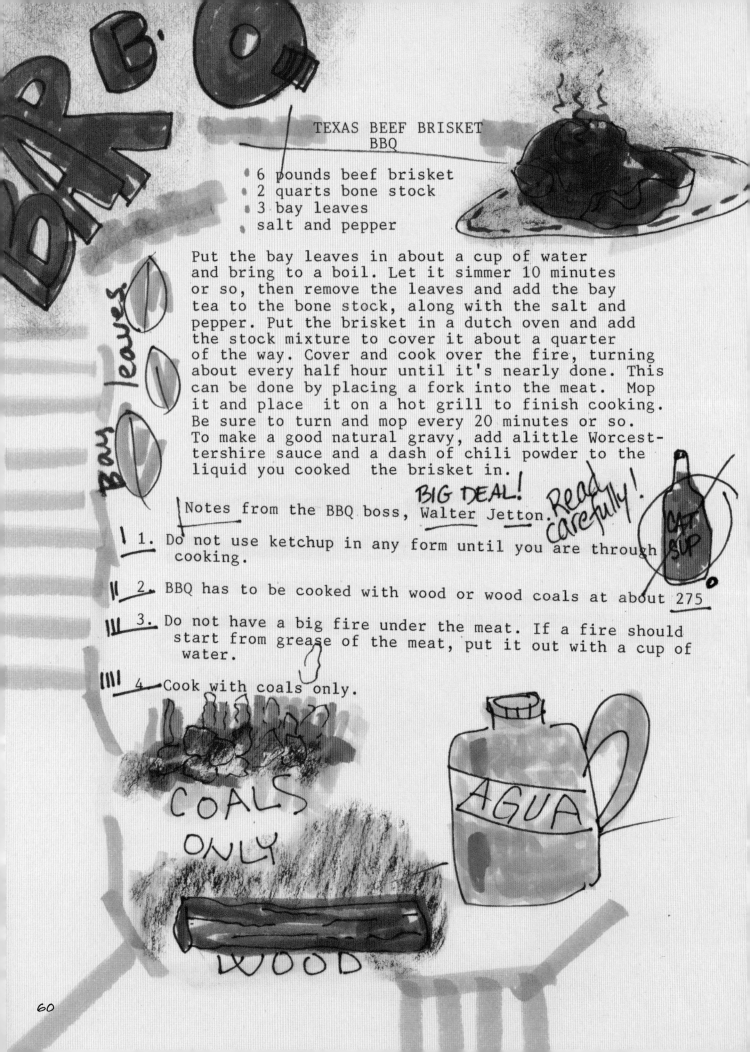

60

RANCH STYLE BEANS

These are the all-time favorite of the Johnson Family.

1 pound dry pinto beans

1/2 pound hog jowl

1 onion, diced

1 small can tomato puree

1 ounce chili peppers

Dash of pepper

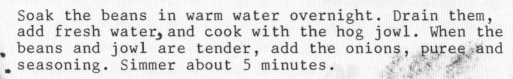

Soak the beans in warm water overnight. Drain them, add fresh water, and cook with the hog jowl. When the beans and jowl are tender, add the onions, puree and seasoning. Simmer about 5 minutes.

Makes 8 good-sized portions.

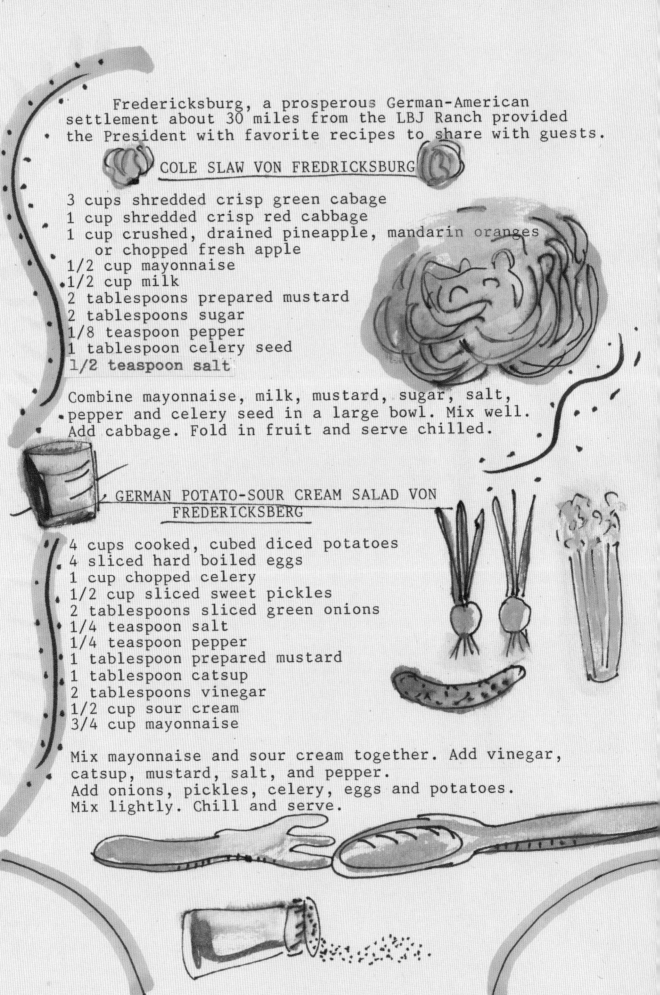

Fredericksburg, a prosperous German-American
settlement about 30 miles from the LBJ Ranch provided
the President with favorite recipes to share with guests.

COLE SLAW VON FREDRICKSBURG

3 cups shredded crisp green cabage
1 cup shredded crisp red cabbage
1 cup crushed, drained pineapple, mandarin oranges
    or chopped fresh apple
1/2 cup mayonnaise
1/2 cup milk
2 tablespoons prepared mustard
2 tablespoons sugar
1/8 teaspoon pepper
1 tablespoon celery seed
1/2 teaspoon salt

Combine mayonnaise, milk, mustard, sugar, salt,
pepper and celery seed in a large bowl. Mix well.
Add cabbage. Fold in fruit and serve chilled.

GERMAN POTATO-SOUR CREAM SALAD VON
FREDERICKSBERG

4 cups cooked, cubed diced potatoes
4 sliced hard boiled eggs
1 cup chopped celery
1/2 cup sliced sweet pickles
2 tablespoons sliced green onions
1/4 teaspoon salt
1/4 teaspoon pepper
1 tablespoon prepared mustard
1 tablespoon catsup
2 tablespoons vinegar
1/2 cup sour cream
3/4 cup mayonnaise

Mix mayonnaise and sour cream together. Add vinegar,
catsup, mustard, salt, and pepper.
Add onions, pickles, celery, eggs and potatoes.
Mix lightly. Chill and serve.

GOOD SO GOOD SO GOOD

Sug·a·r
Sug·a·r

TEXAS COLE SLAW

3 pounds fresh cabbage

2 large dill pickles, chopped

1/2 cup mayonnaise

1/2 cup sugar

1 teaspoon salt

Shred up the cabbage and add all the other ingredients. Mix well and let stand a while before serving so that the flavors get to meet and interact.

20 good-sized portions.

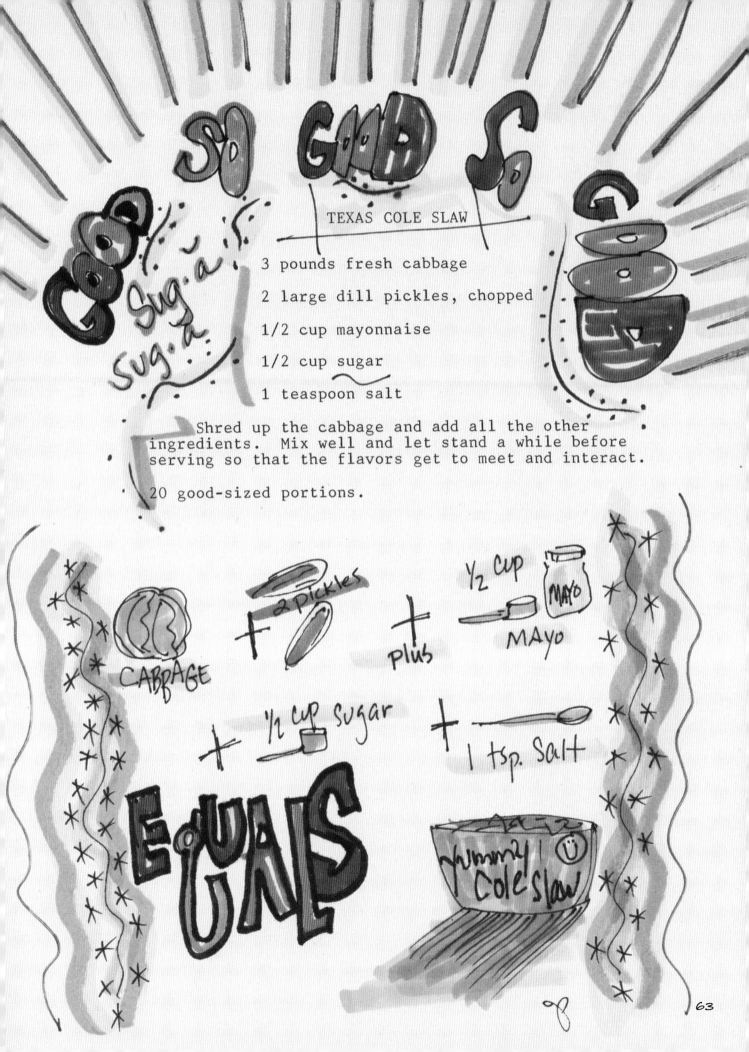

CABBAGE + 2 pickles + Plus ½ cup MAYO

+ ½ cup sugar + 1 tsp. salt

EQUALS

yummy Cole Slaw

es muy especial :)

PRESIDENTIAL SPECIAL

President Johnson's Barbeques Spareribs, with Lady
Bird Johnson's Barbeque Sauce

Bake six pounds of spareribs, cut into three-rib
pieces, for about an hour in a covered pan at 350F,
the day BEFORE the bbq.

Keep chilled until needed.

LADY BIRD JOHNSON BARBEQUE SAUCE:

Quarter cup of butter
- 1/4 cup of vinegar
- 1/4 cup ketchup
- 1/4 cup fresh lemon juice
- 1/4 cup Worcestershire sauce
- 1 onion (chopped)
- 1 clove garlic (minced)
- 1/2 teaspoon salt
- 1/4 teaspoon pepper
- few grains red pepper
- 3 shakes Tabasco sauce

Melt the butter in saucepan, add lemon juice, vinegar,
ketschup, Worcestershire sauce, and spices. Bring to a
boil.
Pour over the ribs to be barbequed and baste from time
to time with mixture.

Grill, turning frequently, until the ribs are crisp
and well done.

Serves 6 to 8

Butter vinager ketchup lemon juice worcestershire sauce
onion (chopped) garlic and salt add pepper red pepper
shake some Tabasco sauce -too!

Walter Jetton named his famous spareribs

Triple-H Spare Ribs

He goes on to say that he named the spare ribs for
Vice-President Hubert H. Humphrey, who gave these ribs
a fit at the Victory BBQ at the LBJ Ranch in November
1964.
He went at them like Clyde Beatty to cats and must
have eaten them for an hour, putting away more of them
than then ever seen, ever. Did him no harm, either.

Like most good dishes, they are easy to fix. Buy the
ribs "two and under," the butcher will know you mean
slabs of ribs two pounds or less in weight.
Sprinkle them with dry rub seasoning, taking care to
get plenty of seasoning under the flap of meat on the
bottom, or bone side, of each slab.
Mop thoroughly and cook on the barbecue grill.

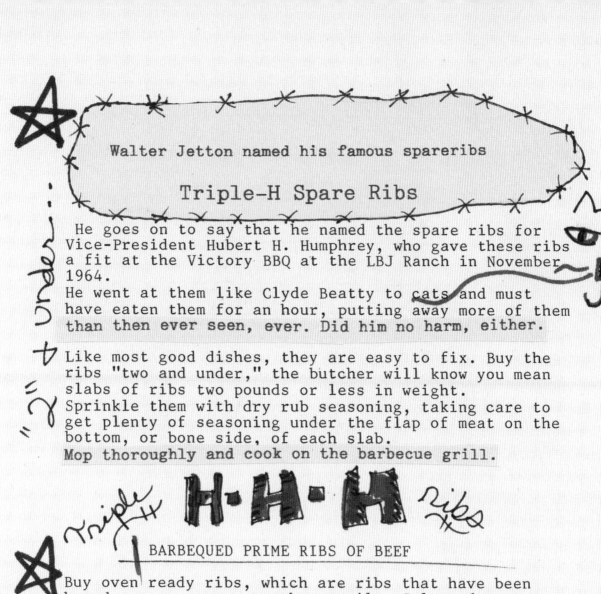

Triple H-H-H ribs

BARBEQUED PRIME RIBS OF BEEF

Buy oven ready ribs, which are ribs that have been
boned so you can carve them easily. Salt and pepper
the roast and lay it on the grill.
Turn it every 20 minutes, using the mop as necessary
to prevent drying.

NURSED VENISON

Dear, I mean Deer meat is a delicacy that people will
talk up a storm about but not really eat. They don't know
how to cook it or they would eat more of it.

Cook a venison roast the same way you would cook a beef
brisket for Texas BBQ. After you put it on the grill, mop
it often (that means nurse it). Use a small mop dipped in your
mop sauce and spread it around on the meat often. This
procedure will alter the gamy taste and the end result
will be something worth eating. (now you tell me)

65

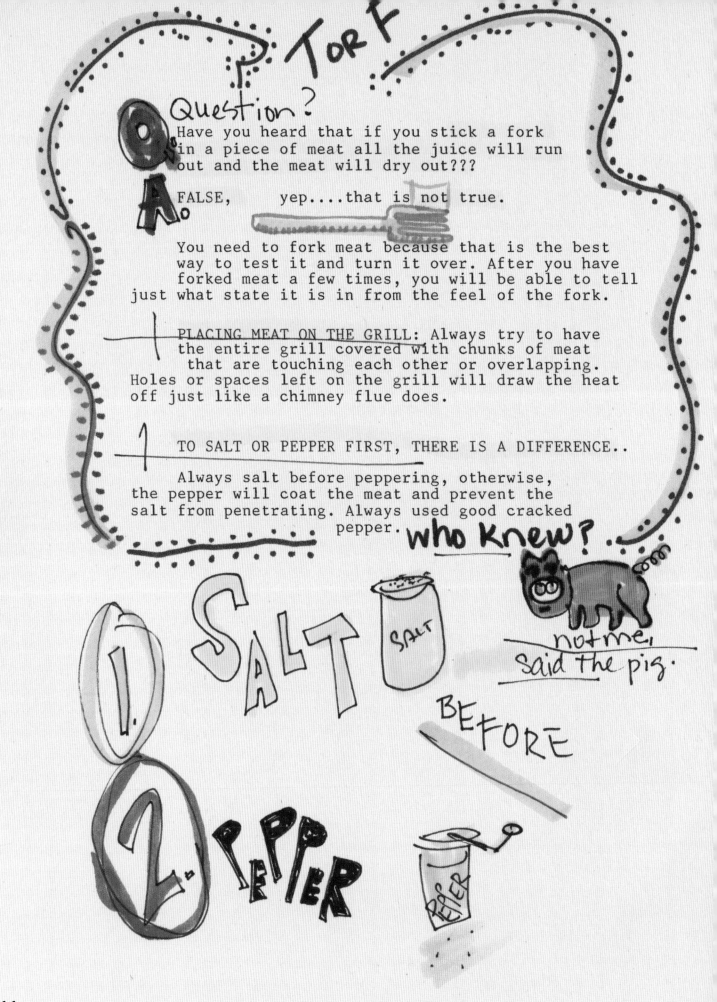

T or F

Question?
Have you heard that if you stick a fork
in a piece of meat all the juice will run
out and the meat will dry out???

A FALSE,   yep....that is not true.

You need to fork meat because that is the best
way to test it and turn it over. After you have
forked meat a few times, you will be able to tell
just what state it is in from the feel of the fork.

PLACING MEAT ON THE GRILL: Always try to have
the entire grill covered with chunks of meat
that are touching each other or overlapping.
Holes or spaces left on the grill will draw the heat
off just like a chimney flue does.

TO SALT OR PEPPER FIRST, THERE IS A DIFFERENCE..

Always salt before peppering, otherwise,
the pepper will coat the meat and prevent the
salt from penetrating. Always used good cracked
pepper. who knew?

not me,
said the pig.

1. SALT
SALT

BEFORE

2. PEPPER
PEPPER

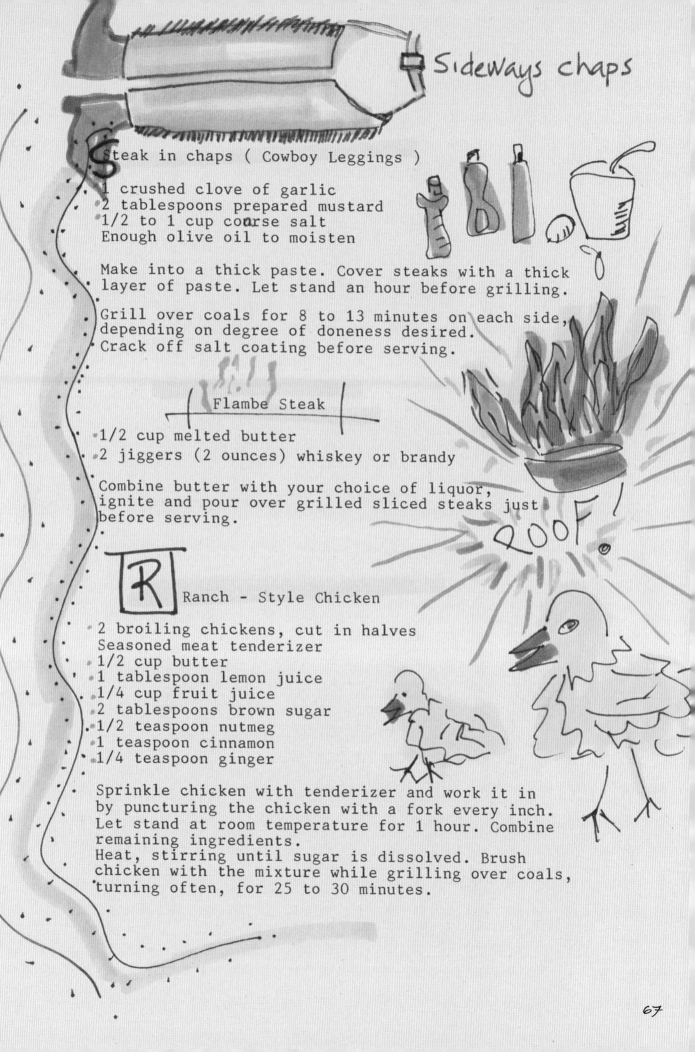

Sideways chaps

Steak in chaps (Cowboy Leggings)

1 crushed clove of garlic
2 tablespoons prepared mustard
1/2 to 1 cup coarse salt
Enough olive oil to moisten

Make into a thick paste. Cover steaks with a thick
layer of paste. Let stand an hour before grilling.

Grill over coals for 8 to 13 minutes on each side,
depending on degree of doneness desired.
Crack off salt coating before serving.

Flambe Steak

1/2 cup melted butter
2 jiggers (2 ounces) whiskey or brandy

Combine butter with your choice of liquor,
ignite and pour over grilled sliced steaks just
before serving.

ROOF!

Ranch - Style Chicken

2 broiling chickens, cut in halves
Seasoned meat tenderizer
1/2 cup butter
1 tablespoon lemon juice
1/4 cup fruit juice
2 tablespoons brown sugar
1/2 teaspoon nutmeg
1 teaspoon cinnamon
1/4 teaspoon ginger

Sprinkle chicken with tenderizer and work it in
by puncturing the chicken with a fork every inch.
Let stand at room temperature for 1 hour. Combine
remaining ingredients.
Heat, stirring until sugar is dissolved. Brush
chicken with the mixture while grilling over coals,
turning often, for 25 to 30 minutes.

! SAGE BRUSH HAMBURGERS !
The best hamburger in the whole wide world

mixture together

1 pound ground beef	2 tablespoons minced onion
1/2 cup milk	3/4 teaspoon salt
1/4 teaspoon pepper	1/2 teaspoon celery salt
1 cup grated sharp cheese	1/2 cup prepared chili sauce
1/4 cup pickle relish	1 tablespoon prepared mustard
3/4 cup chopped olives	1 tablespoon minced onion

Mix together the first 7 ingredients. Shape into 8
thin patties. Combine remaining ingredients. Spread
over four meat patties, and cover with other patties.
Press edges together to seal. Grill on each side 7-10 min.

sagebrush-
A woody plant

Oven-Baked Ribs
with Barbecue Sauce

BBQ Spareribs A la Lady Bird

- Spareribs
- Salt and Pepper
- Canned tomatoes
- Onion
- Garlic
- Worcestershire sauce

- Brown sugar
- Butter
- Ketchup
- Vinegar
- Dry mustard
- Cayenne

Cut the spareribs from 4 racks into manageable sections for eating with the fingers.
Preheat the oven to 350
Place the ribs on a rack in a largish roasting pan.
Sprinkle with salt and pepper and bake for approximately 30 minutes, turning from time to time.
Brush ribs with BBQ sauce and continue baking for another 1/2 hour.
Turn often and brush with sauce.

Smart Lady

"There is no nice way to eat ribs".

-----Lady Bird

BBQ Sauce for A La Lady Bird Spareribs

- 1/4 cup butter
- 1/4 cup catsup
- 1/4 cup Worcestershire
- 1 minced clove garlic
- 1/4 teaspoon pepper
- 1 shake red pepper

- 1/4 cup vinegar
- 1/4 cup lemon juice
- 1 onion (chopped)
- 1/2 teaspoon salt
- 3 or 4 shakes Tabasco Sauce

Melt the butter in the sauce pan, add lemon juice, vinegar, catsup, Worcestershire sauce, chopped onion, garlic and spices. Bring to a boil. Pour over the meat and let sit 20 minutes. Grill the ribs adding sauce frequently. Serves 8.

NOTE: Add the following sides to make the classic BBQ
1. Beans 2. Potato salad 3. Coleslaw 4. onions and dill pickles 5. Fruit cobbler and/or pies.

Beverages

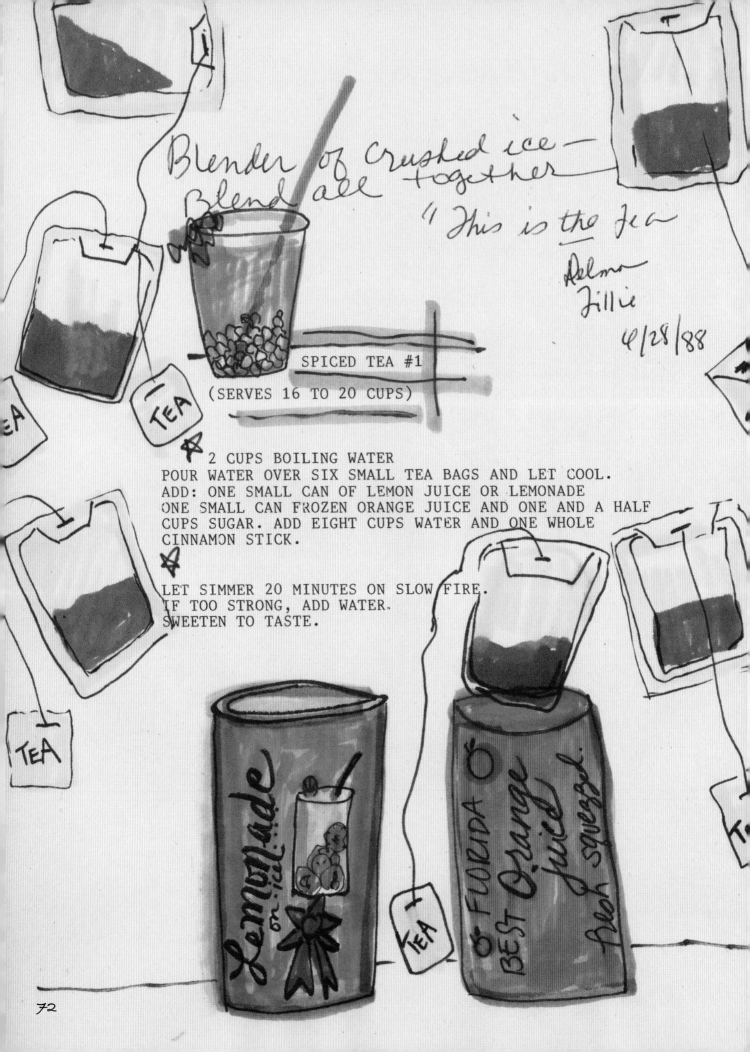

Blender of crushed ice —
Blend all together

"This is the tea

Delma
Fillie
4/28/88

SPICED TEA #1

(SERVES 16 TO 20 CUPS)

2 CUPS BOILING WATER
POUR WATER OVER SIX SMALL TEA BAGS AND LET COOL.
ADD: ONE SMALL CAN OF LEMON JUICE OR LEMONADE
ONE SMALL CAN FROZEN ORANGE JUICE AND ONE AND A HALF
CUPS SUGAR. ADD EIGHT CUPS WATER AND ONE WHOLE
CINNAMON STICK.

LET SIMMER 20 MINUTES ON SLOW FIRE.
IF TOO STRONG, ADD WATER.
SWEETEN TO TASTE.

Lemonade on ice

FLORIDA O BEST Orange juice
fresh squeezed.

TEA

Fruit Punch

Serves 50

2 46-oz. cans unsweetened pineapple juice

1 large can and 1 small can frozen orange
  juice (do not thaw)

2 small cans frozen lemonade or lemon juice

2 small cans frozen lime juice

2 cups sugar

2 large bottles ginger ale

2 large bottles club soda

Mix fruit juices and chill. Just before serving,
add ginger ale and club soda. An ice ring or crushed
ice may be added to keep chilled.

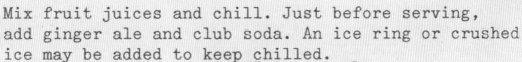

Sangria a la Tom Meyer

Fresh mint

2 measures wine

2 measures orange juice

3/4 measure lemon juice

2 measures soda water

Tear apart fresh mint and rub around the inside of a
jug or pitcher; place torn mint in the bottom. Combine
wine, juices, and soda water and add to the jug. If
too lemony tasting, add sweetener. Add large slices of
fresh peach or orange and lemon slices.

Hot Spiced Punch

1 quart apple cider

3 cinnamon sticks

4 tablespoons lemon juice

1 teaspoon nutmeg

1 teaspoon whole cloves

Simmer cider, cinnamon sticks, and lemon juice for 15 minutes.

Tie nutmeg and cloves in a small cheesecloth bag and put into simmering cider long enough to give it the desired taste.

Serves 8

Wassail----------

1 cup sugar

4 cinnamon sticks

Lemon slices

2 cups pineapple juice

2 cups orange juice

6 cups claret (red wine from Bordeaux)

1/2 cup lemon juice

1 cup dry sherry

Boil sugar, cinnamon sticks, and 3 lemon slices in 1/2 cup water for 5 minutes and strain.

Heat, do not boil the remaining ingredients.

Combine with syrup, garnish with lemon slices, and serve hot.

Banana Daquiri

½ cup lime juice

1 cup Bacardi rum

5 heaping tsp. granulated sugar

½ banana

1 blender pitcher crushed ice

Blend all together.

75

SIX SHOOTER COFFEE

THIS WILL FLOAT A COLT 44....
and is the best coffee ever!!!!

It was made on all chuckwagons,
and just about anything else that
a cowboy would be given to drink,
he would refer to as "bellywash,"
and other names of a similar
complimentary nature.

Now for the directions....drum roll

Put a pound and a half of ground coffee
into a pot with a gallon of water and
boil the hell outta it.
Do not worry about boiling it too long
for there is no such thing.
Set it aside for a few minutes for the
grounds to hit the bottom of the pot
before you pour it.

OR BY THE CUP

For each cup of coffee, combine two
cups cold water, three heaping tablespoons
freshly ground coarse coffee, and a small
pinch of salt. Let water come almost
to a boil. Remove from heat. Do this three
times. Pour gently on the top a little
cold water to settle the coffee grounds.
(Some old timers use crumbled clean egg
shells to settle the grounds and claim
their coffee is clearer).

This according to Chef Walter Jetton, is coffee
that is so strong you can float a .44-revolver on it.
Or, as an old-timer said: "Use coffee and water. When the
coffee boils, toss in iron wedge. If wedge sinks, put in
more coffee."

76

Breads

Whole Wheat Bread

1 yeast cake or one pkg. dry yeast

2 cups lukewarm water

2 Tbsp. sugar

3 1/2 cups white flour

1/2 cup hot water

3 Tablespoons shortening

1/2 cup brown sugar

3 cups whole wheat flour

Dissolve yeast in 1/4 cup warm water. Combine remaining 1 3/4 cups warm water, sugar, salt, and white flour. Add yeast and beat with mixer until smooth.

Let rise until light and bubbly- about 2 hours.

Combine hot water, shortening and sugar. Cool to lukewarm. Add to dough. Beat in whole wheat flour by hand. Knead on floured board. Place in greased bowl. Cover and let rise until about double in size - about 2 hours. Divide into 2 loaves and let rest on board for 15 minutes.

Shape loaf in greased pan and let rise 1 to 1 1/2 hours. Bake at 325F for 45 minutes.

Makes 2 loaves.

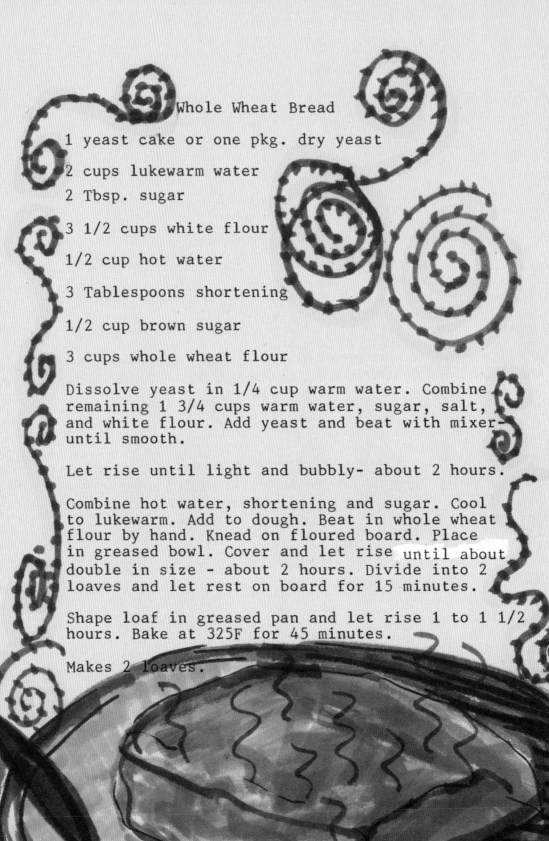

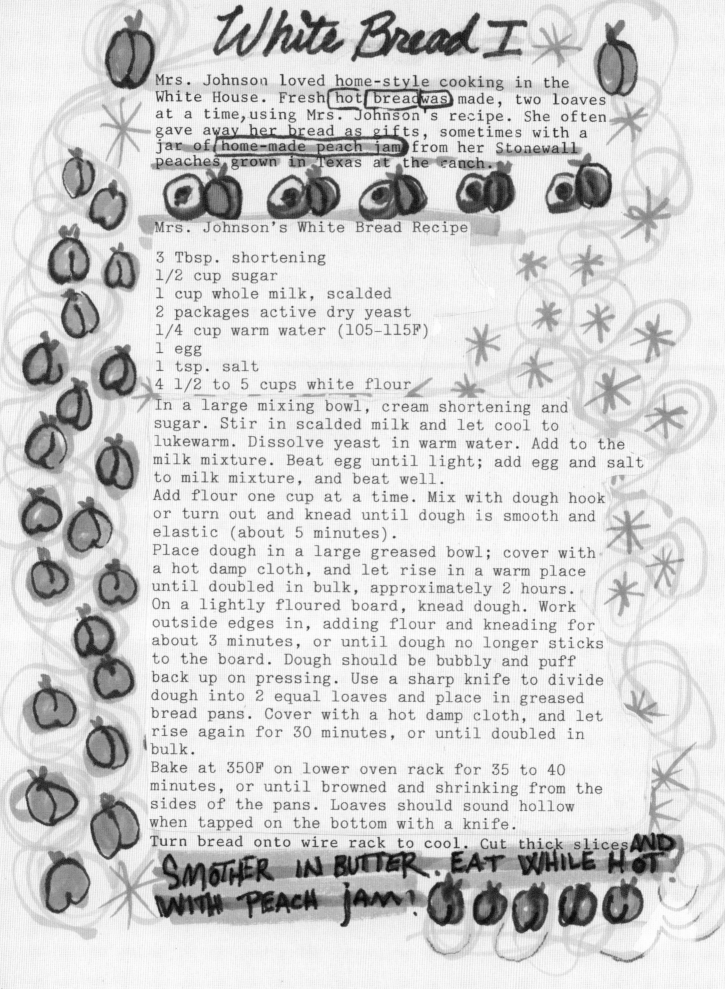

White Bread I

Mrs. Johnson loved home-style cooking in the
White House. Fresh hot bread was made, two loaves
at a time, using Mrs. Johnson's recipe. She often
gave away her bread as gifts, sometimes with a
jar of home-made peach jam from her Stonewall
peaches grown in Texas at the ranch.

Mrs. Johnson's White Bread Recipe

3 Tbsp. shortening
1/2 cup sugar
1 cup whole milk, scalded
2 packages active dry yeast
1/4 cup warm water (105-115F)
1 egg
1 tsp. salt
4 1/2 to 5 cups white flour

In a large mixing bowl, cream shortening and
sugar. Stir in scalded milk and let cool to
lukewarm. Dissolve yeast in warm water. Add to the
milk mixture. Beat egg until light; add egg and salt
to milk mixture, and beat well.
Add flour one cup at a time. Mix with dough hook
or turn out and knead until dough is smooth and
elastic (about 5 minutes).
Place dough in a large greased bowl; cover with
a hot damp cloth, and let rise in a warm place
until doubled in bulk, approximately 2 hours.
On a lightly floured board, knead dough. Work
outside edges in, adding flour and kneading for
about 3 minutes, or until dough no longer sticks
to the board. Dough should be bubbly and puff
back up on pressing. Use a sharp knife to divide
dough into 2 equal loaves and place in greased
bread pans. Cover with a hot damp cloth, and let
rise again for 30 minutes, or until doubled in
bulk.
Bake at 350F on lower oven rack for 35 to 40
minutes, or until browned and shrinking from the
sides of the pans. Loaves should sound hollow
when tapped on the bottom with a knife.
Turn bread onto wire rack to cool. Cut thick slices AND
SMOTHER IN BUTTER. EAT WHILE HOT!
WITH PEACH JAM!

White Bread II

Mrs. Lyndon B. Johnson's
Old Fashion White Bread

1 yeast cake or 1 pkg. dry yeast

1/3 cup warm water

1/4 cup melted shortening

1/2 cup sugar

1 Tbsp. Salt

2 cups lukewarm water

6 cups flour

Dissolve yeast in 1/3 cup warm water. In separate bowl, combine shortening, sugar, salt, and 2 cups lukewarm water. Add yeast. Stir in flour and mix well. Turn onto floured board and knead until smooth. Put dough in greased bowl and let rise until double in size (1-2 hours).

Punch down and shape into two loaves. Put into well-greased bread pans and let rise until double in size (About 40 minutes).

Bake at 350F for 40 to 45 mins.

Makes two loaves.

LBJ'S SPOON BREAD

"Spoon Bread wasone of Lyndon's mother's delightful dishes, "says Mrs. Lyndon B. Johnson, "With a salad (fruit or green) and meat it makes the perfect lunch."

- 3 cups of whole milk
- 3 eggs
- 1 scant cup of corn meal

- chunk of butter the size of a walnut, melted
- 3 teaspoons baking powder
- 1 teaspoon salt

Stir corn meal into 2 cups of milk and let mixture come to a boil, making a mush. Add the remaining milk and well-beaten eggs. Stir in salt, baking powder, and melted butter. Bake 30 minutes at 350F.

Cornbread Muffins

2 1/4 cups yellow cornmeal

1 1/4 cups flour

2 tablespoons baking powder

1/2 teaspoon salt

1/2 teaspoon baking powder

5 tablespoons sugar

4 tablespoons butter, melted

2 eggs

2 1/2 cups buttermilk

6 tablespoons canola oil

1 1/2 cup cups grated cheddar cheese

2 tablespoons canned jalapeños, minced

Preheat oven to 375F. Place cornmeal, flour
baking powder, salt, baking soda, and sugar in a mixing
bowl. Melt butter. In a large mixing bowl, combine eggs,
buttermilk, canola oil, cheddar cheese and jalapeños.
Add dry ingredients to wet ingredients and combine.
Add melted butter and mix well.

To bake: Spray 3 inch muffin tin with pan cooking oil.
Fill muffin pans half full. Bake for 25 minutes or
until golden brown.

Yield 24 muffins.

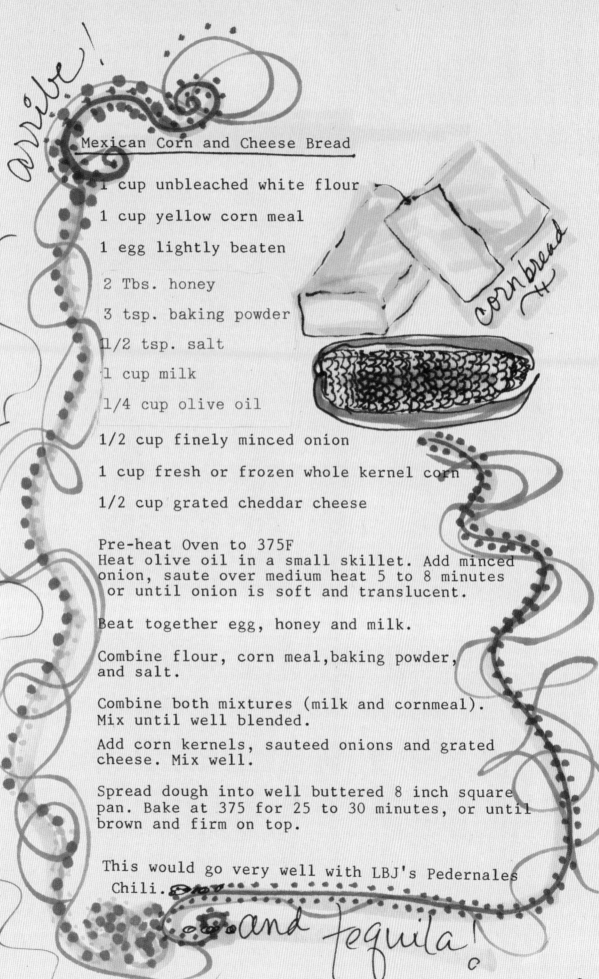

Mexican Corn and Cheese Bread

1 cup unbleached white flour

1 cup yellow corn meal

1 egg lightly beaten

2 Tbs. honey

3 tsp. baking powder

1/2 tsp. salt

1 cup milk

1/4 cup olive oil

1/2 cup finely minced onion

1 cup fresh or frozen whole kernel corn

1/2 cup grated cheddar cheese

Pre-heat Oven to 375F
Heat olive oil in a small skillet. Add minced
onion, saute over medium heat 5 to 8 minutes
or until onion is soft and translucent.

Beat together egg, honey and milk.

Combine flour, corn meal, baking powder,
and salt.

Combine both mixtures (milk and cornmeal).
Mix until well blended.

Add corn kernels, sauteed onions and grated
cheese. Mix well.

Spread dough into well buttered 8 inch square
pan. Bake at 375 for 25 to 30 minutes, or until
brown and firm on top.

This would go very well with LBJ's Pedernales
Chili.

arriba!

cornbread

and tequila!

HUSH PUPPIES

They are good! real good!!

- 2 cups corn meal
- 1/4 cup flour
- 1 egg, beaten
- 2 cups buttermilk
- 6 tablespoons onion, chopped fine
- 1 teaspoon soda
- 1 tablespoon baking powder
- 1 tablespoon salt

Mix all ingredients in a bowl. Take a heaping teaspoon at a time and roll lengthwise between the palms of the hands till you have something that holds together and is shaped like a cigar. These can be long or short, you choose!! Deep fry in hot fat until brown. Drain on paper towels and serve warm.

shh

Let's COOK

Pioneer Corn Pones

"a Southern Version of cornbread"

2 cups cornmeal

1 tsp. salt

3 Tbsp. melted shortening

1 1/2 cups boiling water

Bacon drippings

Mix cornmeal and salt. Stir in melted
shortening, then stir in boiling water. Wet
hands and shape mixture into the shape of
pones (long ovals with the imprint of fingers
on them to resemble ears of corn). Place on a
greased pan and brush tops with bacon
drippings. Bake for 30 minutes in a 375F
oven.

85

President Johnson's Sourdough Biscuits

--makes enough for 4 people.

1 cup of flour

1/4 teaspoon salt

1/2 teaspoon baking soda

2 teaspoons baking powder

1/3 cup cold butter

1 cup sourdough starter

1/2 cup bench flour (bench flour is flour
              sprinkled on the work surface)

sprinkled flour.

Sift together flour, salt, baking powder
              and baking soda. OK?

Cut in the butter

Mix in sourdough starter

Turn out dough onto lightly floured (bench flour)
board.

Knead a few times, until all of the flour
is worked into the dough ←takes muscle.

Roll out dough to about 3/4 inch thick and cut
out biscuits. Place on ungreased baking sheet.

Bake at 425F for 12 to 15 minutes, or until
biscuits are golden-brown on top.

LBJ loved these!

J.

my sourdough. * But do not fool with * Mess with my wife * Mess with my life * You may ruin my life

*Here lies Bigfoot Joe
He was our friend * Messed with the sourdough *
that was the END!

BIG FOOT JOE

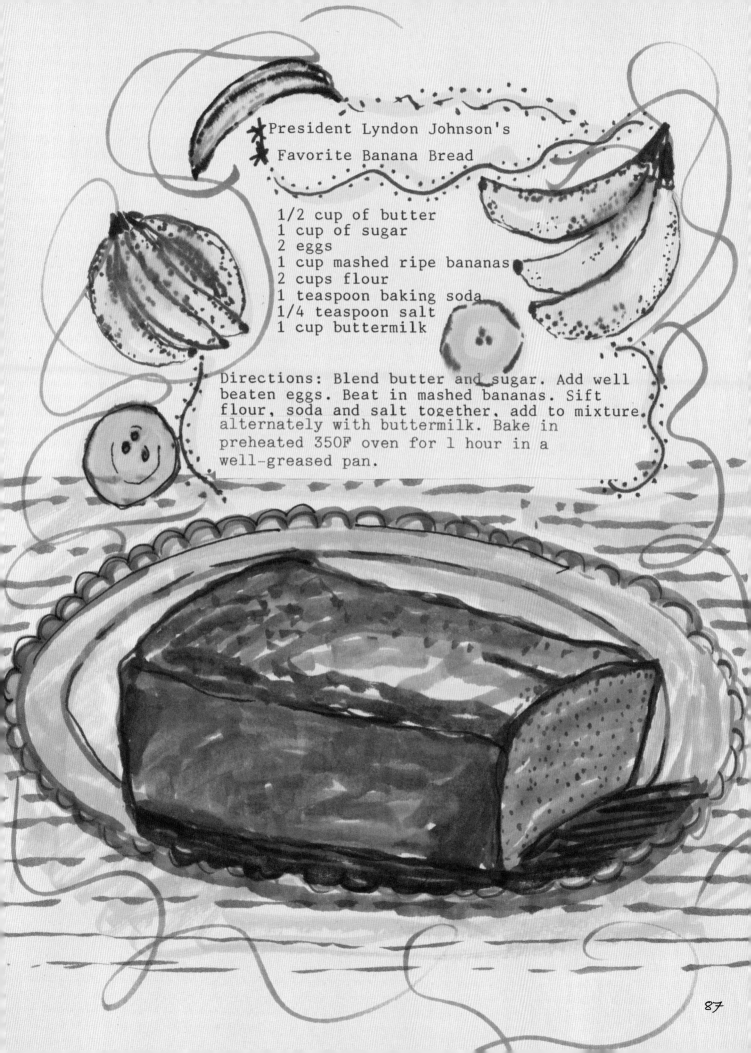

President Lyndon Johnson's
Favorite Banana Bread

1/2 cup of butter
1 cup of sugar
2 eggs
1 cup mashed ripe bananas
2 cups flour
1 teaspoon baking soda
1/4 teaspoon salt
1 cup buttermilk

Directions: Blend butter and sugar. Add well
beaten eggs. Beat in mashed bananas. Sift
flour, soda and salt together, add to mixture
alternately with buttermilk. Bake in
preheated 350F oven for 1 hour in a
well-greased pan.

RAISIN

Lynda Robb's Recipe

for

Raisin Bran Bread

1 large box raisins
2 teaspoons baking soda
1 tablespoon shortening
2 cups sugar
1 tsp. salt
1 tsp. cinnamon
4 cups flour
2 beaten eggs
1 teaspoon vanilla

In a large bowl mix raisins with 2 cups boiling water. Let stand one hour.
Sift together all dry ingredients. Mix in eggs, vanilla, raisins, and raisin water.
Do NOT beat.
Fill greased loaf pans 3/4 full.
Bake at 350F for 50 to 60 minutes.
Makes 2 loaves.

BRAN BREAD

Moncrief Monkey Bread

1 cup milk, scalded
1 cup mashed potatoes
2/3 cup shortening
1 tsp. salt
2/3 cup sugar

1 yeast cake
1/2 cup lukewarm water
2 eggs, well beaten
5 to 6 cups flour
Melted butter

Combine milk, potatoes, shortening, salt and sugar in a large bowl. Let stand until lukewarm. Dissolve yeast in warm water; add to potato mixture. Stir in eggs. Add 1 1/2 cup flour; beat well. Continue to add flour until dough is stiff. Turn out on floured board and knead thoroughly. Place in greased bowl. Brush oil over top of dough, and cover loosely. Let rise 2 hours. Put in refrigeratator to chill. About an hour before serving time, roll out dough to 1/2 inch thick. Cut into dough a shape of 2 inch diamonds and pull dough to stretch diamonds to elongate. Cut diamonds in both ends. Then repeat until dough is all cut into diamond shapes. Dip diamond shapes into butter. Arrange a layer of diamonds in a well-buttered, 2-quart ring mold. Arrange a second layer of diamonds on top of the first, staggering diamonds so that the seams do not align. Continue layering dough until half is used. Repeat in second pan until dough is used up.

Let rise until double in size at least one hour.
Bake at 400 for 20 to 25 minutes.
Makes 2 rings.

Mrs. John H. Meyers
Alice Baker Jones

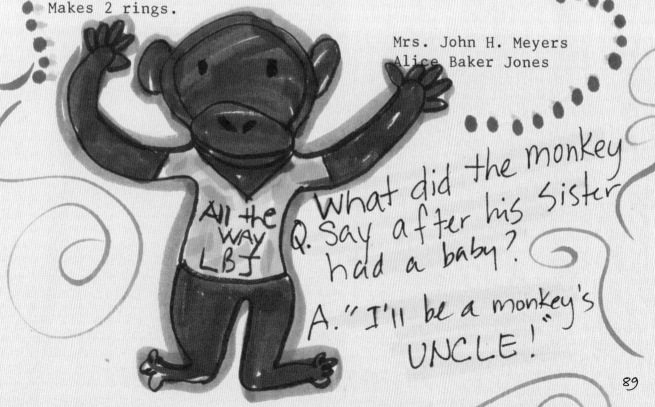

What did the monkey
Q. Say after his Sister
had a baby?

A. "I'll be a monkey's
UNCLE!"

At the
White House

LBJ really wanted to be the President of the

United States

--At some point in his career JOhnson
realized he just wasn't what he needed
to be to actually be the President.
So...he began to consider the second spot.

He had his staff look up how many presidents
in the last hundred years had died in office.

A. Seven

1. John Tyler (upon William Henry Harrison's
death in 1841)

2. Millard Fillmore (upon Zachary Taylor's
death in 1850)

3. Andrew Johnson (upon Abraham Lincoln's
assassination)

4. Chestor A. Arthur (upon James Garfield's
assassination 1881)

5. Theodore Roosevelt (upon William McKinley's
assassination in 1901)

6. Calvin Coolidge (upon Warren Harding's
death in 1923)

7. Harry Truman (upon Franklin Roosevelt's
death in 1945)

When Clare Boothe Luce asked LBJ why he would
consider being number two / why he would accept
the nomination of being number 2./LBJ responded,
" Clare, I looked it up; one out of every four
Presidents has died in office. I'm a gamblin'
man, darlin', and this is the only chance I got."

Kennedy wanted LBJ because he was a master of
southern politics. (It worked out!)

"Shit, shit, shit."

—Bobby Kennedy

*after Jack told Bobby he was asking LBJ
to be his running mate.

from John Loengard: <u>Life</u>
<u>Photographers</u>: <u>What They Saw</u>

Kennedy and Johnson had an agreement that if Kennedy became incapacitated and could no longer serve, he would tell Johnson, who would then assume the presidency. If Kennedy was unable to communicate with Johnson, then Johnson could assume the powers of the presidency after consulting the Cabinet. The president could resume the presidency whenever he decided he was able to do so.

Article II of the Constitution provided a Succession Clause stating that "In Case of the Removal of the President from Office, or of his Death, Resignation, or inability to discharge the Powers and Duties of the said Office, the Same shall devolve on the Vice President..." The remaining text of the article, however, was unclear regarding how long the vice president was to perform such duties, and although vice presidents regularly succeeded presidents who died in office, the clause caused years of legal debate over the matter. It was not until its ratification on February 10, 1967, that the Twenty-Fifth Amendment settled the issue by stating flatly that "In case of the removal of the President from office or his death or resignation, the Vice-President shall become President." It also listed the order of succession in case the vice president was also unable to fulfill presidential duties.

In a nutshell:

In a nutshell...

Johnson spent ten hours and nineteen minutes alone with Kennedy in their first

1st

year in office. The third year they spent one hour and fifty-three minutes together.

3rd

At JFK's surprise forty-sixth birthday party on May 29, 1963, Johnson wasn't there because nobody invited him---ooppps. No one "remembered" to ring him up.

Johnson later found out!

— yikes —

Upon learning that no one remembered to invite him. Johnson yelled, "I'd like to get out of this damn town, go back to Texas and never come back!"

Friday, November 22, 1963

The front-page banner headline for the Washington Post
EXTRA

President Kennedy Shot Dead

By Assassin in Dallas Parade

Kennedy's car raced through the streets to
Parkland Hospital. Secret Service to Johnson:
"You and Mrs. Johnson stick with me and the
other agents as close as you can...We are
going into the hospital and we aren't gonna
stop for anything or anybody. Do you
understand?"

Twelve minutes after being wheeled into
trauma room 1, Kennedy was pronounced dead.

The president's remains were transported back
to Washington, DC, on Air Force One, along
with Mrs. Kennedy, the Johnsons, and the rest
of the presidential entourage. This was the
first time Johnson was ever on Air Force One.
Johnson requested a glass of water and a cup
of hot vegetable soup.

Johnson called Rose Kennedy from the plane's
conference room. "Mrs. Kennedy, I wish to God
there was something I could do for you." He
passed the phone to Lady Bird.

Johnson then called Bobby Kennedy.

I've often wondered exactly where Mr. Johnson
was when he found out he was the President of the United
States.

Here is what I found from a file in the archives from the
LBJ Library. I am quoting page 12 from a Secret Service report

"We later found out that he (Mr. Johnson) sat in a little
room off of the emergency room. I think it was one of
these little examining rooms. He sat on the examining
table and his wife on a wooden stool next to him, with just
a Secret Service agent at the door. That's where he was
while he became President."

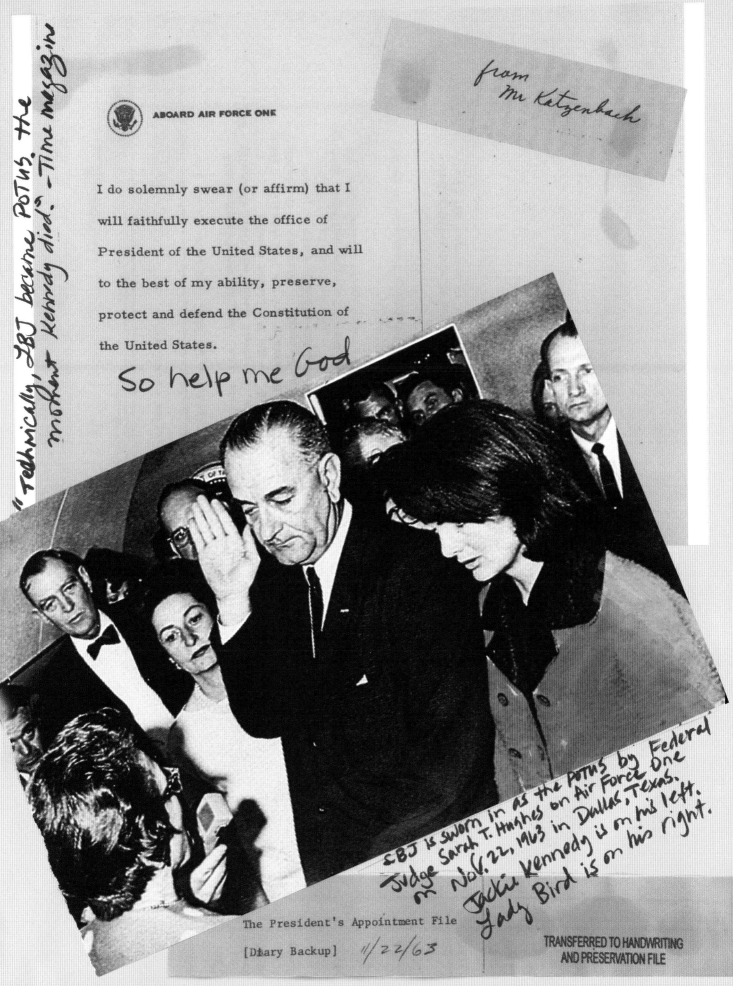

"technically," LBJ became POTUS the moment Kennedy died." —Time magazine

ABOARD AIR FORCE ONE

from
Mr Katzenbach

I do solemnly swear (or affirm) that I
will faithfully execute the office of
President of the United States, and will
to the best of my ability, preserve,
protect and defend the Constitution of
the United States.

So help me God

LBJ is sworn in as the POTUS by Federal
Judge Sarah T. Hughes on Air Force One
on Nov. 22, 1963 in Dallas, Texas.
Jackie Kennedy is on his left.
Lady Bird is on his right.

The President's Appointment File

[Diary Backup]   11/22/63

TRANSFERRED TO HANDWRITING
AND PRESERVATION FILE

99

The pink wool suit Jacqueline Kennedy wore
that day was a design from Coco Chanel's
Fall-Winter 1961 collection.

"Although the design was by Chanel, the suit
itself was fitted and sewn for the First Lady
in New York by high-end Manhattan boutique
Chez Nino, with fabrics, buttons, and trim
directly sent from the Chanel atelier in
Paris. This was due to Kennedy's political
position at the time. It was only acceptable
for First Ladies to be seen in American-made
clothing..."
                                    —Ella Faust

There is caked blood all over Jackie. After
they are on Air Force One, Lady Bird asks
Jackie if she wants to change. Jackie says
NO, I want them to see what they have done to
Jack.

They need to find a Bible.

LBJ wants to be sworn in by Judge Sarah T.
Hughes, who was a long-time friend. A
Catholic missal is found in JFK's side table
in his bedroom on Air Force One. It is in a
small box wrapped in cellophane. The box is
torn open, and the missal is handed to Judge
Hughes.

2:38 p.m. LBJ is sworn in as POTUS.
It has been 98 minutes since JFK died.

2:41 p.m.
Johnson issues his first official directive
as POTUS:
        "Let's get airborne."

November 26
Tuesday
Dear Mr. President,

Letter from Jackie-O after "The" funeral.

Thank you for walking yesterday- behind Jack. You did not have to do that- I am sure many people forbid you to take such a risk- but you did it anyway.

Thank you for your letters to my children. What those letters will mean to them later- you can imagine. The touching thing is, they have always loved you so much, they were most moved to have a letter from you now.

And most of all, Mr. President, thank you for the way you have always treated me- the way you and Lady Bird have always been to me-before, when Jack was alive, and now as President.

I think the relationship of the Presidential and Vice-Presidential families could be a rather strained one. From the history I have been reading ever since I came to the White House, I gather it often was in the past.

But you were Jack's right arm - and I always thought the greatest act of a gentleman that I had seen on this earth- was how you- the Majority Leader when he came to the Senate as just another little freshman who looked up to you and took orders from you, could then serve as Vice President to a man who had served under you and been taught by you.

But more than we were friends, all four of us. All you did for me as a friend and the happy times we had. I always thought way before the nomination that Lady Bird should be First Lady- but I don't need to tell you here what I think of her qualities- her extraordinary grace of character- her willingness to assume every burden- She assumed so many for me and I love her very much- and I love your two daughters- Lynda Bird most because I know her the best- and we first met when neither of us could get a seat to hear President Eisenhower's State of the Union message, and someone found us a place on one of the steps on the aisle where we sat together. If we had known then what our relationship would be now.

It was so strange-last night I was wandering through this house. There in the Treaty Room is your chandelier, and I had framed- the page we all signed-you- Senator Dirksen and Mike Mansfield- underneath I had written "The day the Vice-President brought the East Room chandelier back from the Capitol."

1.

Then in the library I showed Bobby the Lincoln Record book you gave-you see all you gave-and now you are called on to give so much more.

Your office- you are the first President to sit in it as it looks today. Jack always wanted a red rug- and I had curtains designed for it that I thought were as dignified as they should be for a President's office.

Late last night a moving man asked me if I wanted Jack's ship pictures left on the wall for you (They were clearing the office to make room for you) - I said no because I remembered all the fun Jack had those first days hanging pictures of things he loved, setting out his collection of whales teeth etc.

But of course they are there only waiting for you to ask for them if the walls look too bare. I thought you would want to put things from Texas in it- I pictured some gleaming longhorns- I hope you put them somewhere.

It mustn't be very much help to you your first day in office - to hear children on the lawn at recess. It is just one more example of your kindness that you let them stay- I promise- they will soon be gone-
Thank you Mr. President

Respectfully,

Jackie

https:blogs.mprnews.org/newscut/2013/11/a-letter-from-jackie/

NOTE: I think Jackie was referring to Caroline Kennedy's kindergarten class that was situated in the White House Solarium. There were 20 students in the class and recess was on the lawn of the White House. The Kennedys and the other parents paid the teacher's salary and the school met regulations set by the District of Columbia.

2.

Johnson assessed his first 100

days

in an interview on March 15, 1964

he said:

"The first priority was to try to
display to the world that we could
have continuity and transition, that
the program of President Kennedy would
be carried on, that there was no need
for them to be disturbed and fearful
that our constitutional system had
been endangered. To demonstrate to the
people of this country that although their
leader had fallen, and we had a new
president, that we must have unity and we
we must close ranks, and we must work
together for the good of all America and
the world."

...And that is that!

REST ROOMS
WHITE   COLORED

President Johnson's awareness of the difficulties Zephyr wright experienced traveling through the segregated South- the hardship and humiliation of not being served in restaurants on the road, the difficulty of finding accommodations- are believed to have influenced his work on civil rights reform and legislation.

maids in white uniforms ——PERMITTED——

NO IRISH
NO BLACKS
NO DOGS

WAITING ROOM
FOR COLORED ONLY
——————→
By order
Police Dept.

WHITE ONLY

WE WANT WHITE TENANTS IN OUR WHITE COMMUNITY

Imperial Laundry Co. We Wash for WHITE PEOPLE ONLY

WE SERVE WHITE'S —NO only— SPANISH or MEXICANS—

WHITES ONLY!

WE CATER TO WHITE TRADE ONLY

JIM CROW LAWS WRITTEN and ENFORCED by the DEMOCRATIC PARTY 1876 - 1965

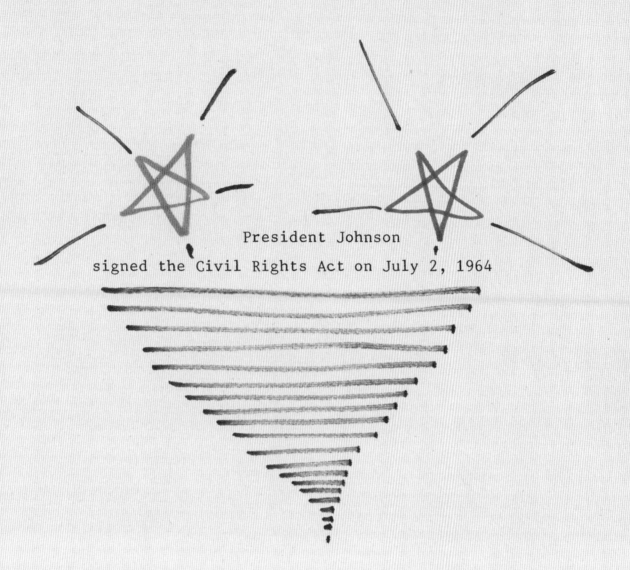

President Johnson
signed the Civil Rights Act on July 2, 1964

1964 the big campaign year!!!

The train trip to the South!!!!

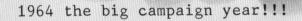
According to Bess Abell,

"Johnson had taken a train trip through the South as a candidate for vice president in '60, and alot of the very wise heads in the Democratic Party didn't want the Johnsons to go into the South. They felt like this was the part of the country that he was going to lose anyway, and why make the effort!

"I think Mrs. Johnson felt very strongly about this, and I think the President too. This is the part of the country that they're associated with, and they didn't want to write it off, all the Democrats down there were working for the party and for them. They just didn't want to say, "This is a part of the country and we've just X'ed through it, because there's nothiung in it for us."

"The train trips involved an unbelievable number of people. It started out with an advance team of, which Liz Carpenter and Joe Moran, who was the head of the advance men, and the Secret Service and probably the communications people took in a plane, which was going to alot of big cities. And then we sent out about ten or so advance women*who would just move into a town and stay for two or three weeks. And then there was a team of advance men who went out to each town."

*the women -on the advance team were:
Judith Moyers, Bill Moyers's wife.
She ended up in New Orleans.

Lindy Boggs, Mrs. Hale Boggs--the congressman's
  wife from Louisiana.

Cara Burney, a friend of Mrs, Johnson's from
  Texas.

"I don't have that list in my mind to pull out
  but these woman went out to each of these
    little towns."

"One of the assignments that fell my way was
working on a food train and the cars for the trains
and the balloons and the give away items, working with

the hostesses. It was really quite a major undertaking,
and what I kept looking for was that last car, just a
car that wouldn't have any partitions in it and would
also have a big back platform on it.

We were told that there wasn't such a thing;
that those cars just went out with bustles, were NOT
available.

I mentioned it to the President one night and he said,
"It's just vital."

We called and we visited and we toured around all
the railroad yards, and it just wasn't available.
Then the President called me one Sunday and he said,
"You call Buford Ellington"--who is now governor of
Tennessee but at that time was working with one of the
railroads, I think L&N---"you call Buford and he'll
find you that car."

So I called Buford, and he said, "I never heard of a
car like that in this day and age, but we'll see if
we can find it." He called me later that night, or
maybe early Monday morning, and said, "They've found
one over in Pittsburgh, or Philadelphia, on the junk
heap, and they're going to put it on the back of a
train and get it down to Washington for you this
afternoon."

So we went down to see the train and it really was in
shambles, but it was exactly what we wanted--just an
empty car with a great big platform on the back. We
had a nice architect come down and design us a striped
awning   for the back of it and took one of the
calligraphers from the White House down and he drew
up the side of the train and how we wanted it painted,
red, white, and blue. I got the upholsterer who worked

The train trip to the South/ Page 3
from: Bess Abell, Social Secretary/ Oral History
page 12 con't

....on putting fine silks on all the White House
furnishings to go and buy the cheapest red and
blue cotton he could find and recover all the seats,
and we painted it blue on the inside and tacked up
pictures of the Johnsons campaigning, and it was
just great!.
It was also very hot. The car, as I said, was really
off the junk heap and it did not have any modern air
conditioning facilities and had to be air-conditioned
with ice.
One of the additional jobs of the advance men at each
of these stops was to get the iceman to load the ice
on the base of the train, so as soon as we pulled
into a station somebody out there in the crowd was
assigned to load the ice aboard to keep us going
till the next stop.

Question to Ms. Abell..."Did any of the male politicians
                        worry about the females running
                        this show?"

Answer: Oh, Yes!!! Kenny O'Donnell- I don't know
whether that's true of Larry O'Brien, less so, I
think, but they didn't want Mrs. JOhnson to do anything. They were really just opposed to it. I think
all of that is just what kind of women you're used to
and what kind of respect you have for them--I really
think that they thought Mrs. Johnson coudn't make a
contribution. They didn't know any women like her."

[Mrs. Johnson received many gifts along the way, and there wasn't room to store anything.]

...We had to get rid of all the stuff that was given to Mrs. Johnson, or we would have had to add a number of cars to the train, and it was plenty long enough. People would meet Mrs. Johnson and want to have their picture taken with her and give her a gift, like a bouquet of flowers or a homemade cake or a bushel of apples or a mincemeat pie.

The Secret Service was such a bear about the food; they made us throw away all the food for fear somebody----we could eat it on the train if we wanted to, but Mrs. Johnson or Lynda or Luci weren't allowed to have that food, but the rest of us---if we decided to take a chance they really didn't quarrel, although they didn't approve.

I recall the well-publicized episode of a picket or a heckler of some kind whom Mrs. Johnson handled very well with her statement about "It's tme now for me to have my say," or something to that effect.

Yes. "You've had yours, now it's time for me to have mine. In this country we hear all views. I've heard yours, and now I want you to be polite and hear mine." That worked a couple of places. It was not successful in -Charleston. It was wherever Mendell Rivers was. But I thought his speech was ghastly anyway."

We had over 150 press, we had European press traveling with us. One of the classic stories of the trip is that two French reporters who got on were not seen again until we arrived in New Orleans.

They were on the train, but we never saw them. Just gave them a free ride.

It was a remarkable trip, but we lost all the states.

There is a different side to the
story of that whistle stop
campaign.

"I cannot all these years later do justice to
what she faced: The boos, the jeers, the
hecklers, the crude signs and cruder gestures,
the insults and the threats....
Rumors spread of snipers, and in the panhandle of
Florida the threats are so ominous the FBI orders
a yard-by-yard sweep of a 7-mile bridge that her
train would cross. She never flinches. Up to 40
times a day from the platform of the caboose she
will speak, sometimes raising a single white-
gloved hand to punctuate her words, always the
lady. When the insults grew so raucous in South
Carolina, she tells the crowd the ugly words were
coming 'not from the good people of South
Carolina but from the state of confusion.' In
Columbia she answers hecklers with what one
observer called 'a maternal bark.' And she says,
'This is a country of many viewpoints. I respect
your right to express your own. Now it is my turn
to express mine.'"

—Bill Moyers

From remarks made at a memorial service for Lady
Bird in 2007. Source: govinfo.gov CDOC-
11sdoc8.pdf. Accessed 3/24/22

Moyers was Special Assistant to Lyndon Johnson
from 1963 to 1967.

P.S. Please don't forget to vote on Nov. 3 — Lady Bird Johnson

Washington

Raleigh

Charleston

Tallahassee

New Orleans

Lady Bird Special

January 20, 1965
Time 12:03

LBJ's Inaugural in DC
The constitution states that the presidential
term shall end at 12 noon on January 20th.

Therefore, technically the U.S.A. had no
President for three minutes.

Words in LBJ's Inaugural address - 1507
Applause's - 11

The nation had been without a Vice President
for 14 months.

The Speaker of the House John McCormack had
been next in line to be the President.

Security at the parade was so tight that the
Cochiti Indian Tribal dancers from New Mexico
were asked to remove the points from their
arrows. They did indeed.

The presidential limousine was the one used
by JFK, it had been fitted with a non-removable
bullet-proof bubbletop and armor plated sides.
An armor plate was built into the floor to
withstand a bomb attack.

He was the first president since George Washington
to dance at his own inaugural Ball. He danced
with his wife and changed partners nine times
in fifteen minutes.

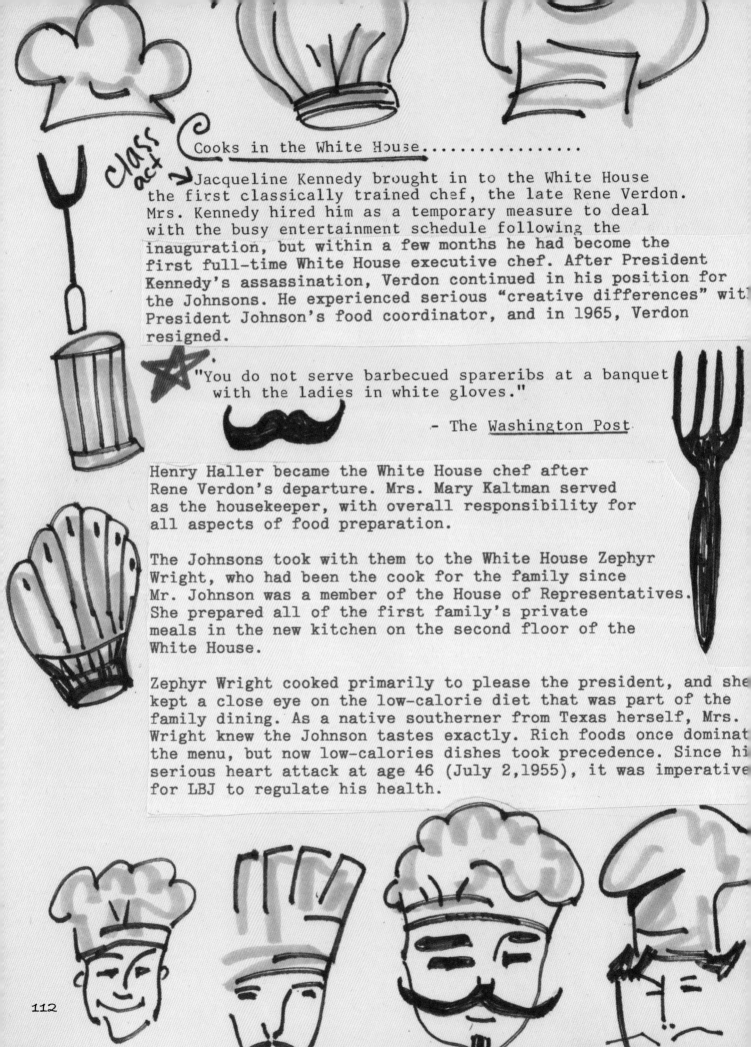

Cooks in the White House.................

Jacqueline Kennedy brought in to the White House
the first classically trained chef, the late Rene Verdon.
Mrs. Kennedy hired him as a temporary measure to deal
with the busy entertainment schedule following the
inauguration, but within a few months he had become the
first full-time White House executive chef. After President
Kennedy's assassination, Verdon continued in his position for
the Johnsons. He experienced serious "creative differences" with
President Johnson's food coordinator, and in 1965, Verdon
resigned.

"You do not serve barbecued spareribs at a banquet
        with the ladies in white gloves."

                                    - The Washington Post

Henry Haller became the White House chef after
Rene Verdon's departure. Mrs. Mary Kaltman served
as the housekeeper, with overall responsibility for
all aspects of food preparation.

The Johnsons took with them to the White House Zephyr
Wright, who had been the cook for the family since
Mr. Johnson was a member of the House of Representatives.
She prepared all of the first family's private
meals in the new kitchen on the second floor of the
White House.

Zephyr Wright cooked primarily to please the president, and she
kept a close eye on the low-calorie diet that was part of the
family dining. As a native southerner from Texas herself, Mrs.
Wright knew the Johnson tastes exactly. Rich foods once dominated
the menu, but now low-calories dishes took precedence. Since his
serious heart attack at age 46 (July 2,1955), it was imperative
for LBJ to regulate his health.

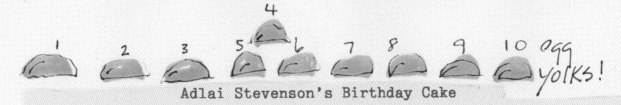

1 2 3 4 5 6 7 8 9 10 egg yolks!

Adlai Stevenson's Birthday Cake

On February 5, 1965, the United Nations Ambassador, Adlai Stevenson, had a meeting at the White House with the president. At the end of the meeting, Lady Bird Johnson appeared with a cake that had white icing and one candle, to commemorate Stevenson's sixty-fifth birthday.

It was a sponge cake filled and covered with candied-fruit-spangled whipped cream.

Recipe for Adlai's Birthday Cake

Ingredients

Egg yolks   Candied fruit, diced
Hot water   Baking powder
Sugar   salt
Almond extract   heavy cream, whipped
Cake flour

    Preheat oven to 325F. Beat 10 egg yolks in a large bowl, gradually adding 1/2 cup hot water. Beat until almost double in volume. Continue beating as you gradually add 1 cup sugar. Add 1 teaspoon almond extract. Sift together 1 2/3 cups cake flour, 1/2 tsp. baking powder, 1/2 tsp. salt. Fold the sifted ingredients into yolk mixture, one-fourth at a time, with a rubber spatula or wire whisk. Line bottoms of two deep 9-inch pans with waxed paper. Pour batter into pans and bake 30 to 40 minutes, or until golden brown. Invert pans to cool.

Frosting:
    Whip 1 pint heavy cream until stiff. Combine 1 cup whipped cream with 1/2 cup diced candied fruit. Spread between layers. Cover top and sides with remaining whipped cream. Sprinkle candied fruit on top. Refrigerate until ready to serve. Serves 10.

whipping heavy cream for the frosting

HAPPY BIRTHDAY!!
Adlai!
JS

113

Vietnam and the V.P.

On Feb. 17 1965, VP Hubert Humphrey sent LBJ a memorandum stating the USA must begin an exit strategy in Vietnam:

"It is always hard to cut losses. But the Johnson administration is in a stronger position to do so now than any administration in this century."

Johnson had trounced Barry Goldwater in the 1964 election--and thus, no longer had to prove he was tough on Communism-- and the conflict had not developed into a full-blown war.

"Nineteen sixty-five is the year of minimum political risk," Humphrey wrote.

But Johnson refused his advice.

Humphrey was removed from the spotlight and the decision making process. In August 1965, the comedian and musician Tom Lehrer sang to a raucous audience.

WHATEVER BECAME OF YOU, HUBERT?

whatever became of you Hubert?
we miss you, so tell us, please:
are you sad? are you cross?

are you gathering moss?

while you wait for the boss to sneeze?

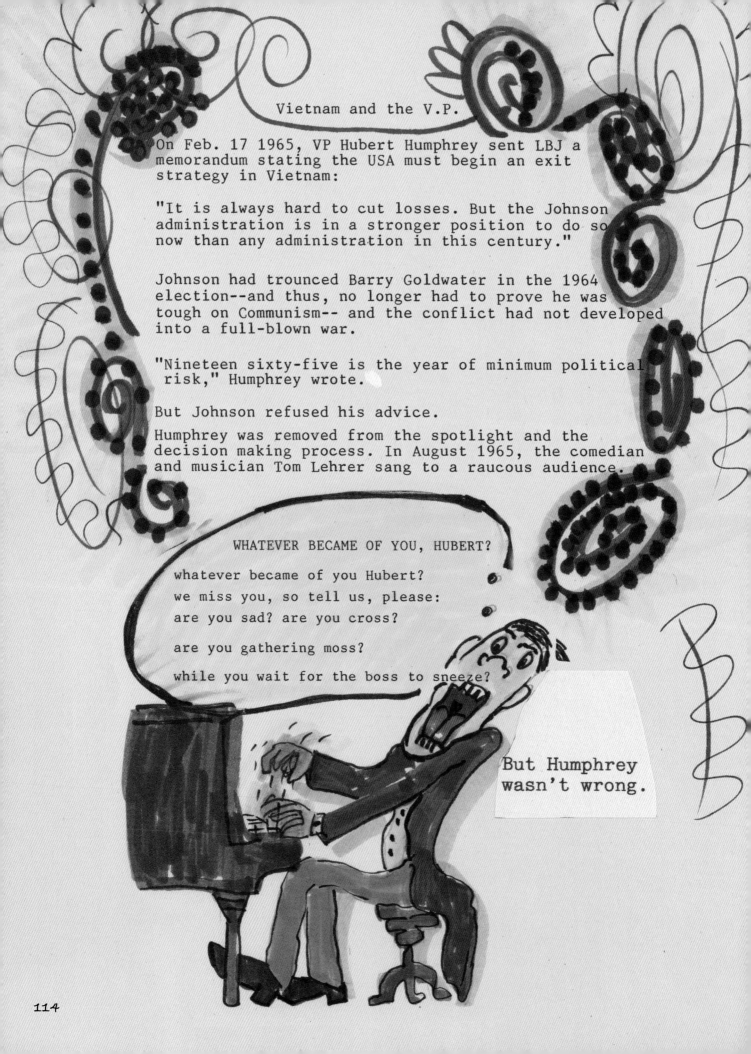

But Humphrey wasn't wrong.

A PERFECT STORM

LBJ understood the dangers of Vietnam well before the election.

"I don't think it's worth fighting for, and I don't think we can get out ... It's just the biggest damned mess that I ever saw."

Johnson was elected by a landslide in 1964, defeating Barry Goldwater with 61 percent of the vote—the largest popular referendum since 1820. He and Lady Bird attended 5 inaugural balls.

By 1968, he had reached the nadir of his popularity. Massive protests against the Vietnam War had spread not only across the US but around the world.

On the night of March 31, 1968, Johnson concluded a national televised speech to the nation that he wouldn't seek reelection.

Unrest continued.

Martin Luther King Jr. was assassinated four days later. Riots and increased civil rights protests followed.

Robert F. Kennedy was assassinated two months later. The senator was shot in Los Angeles while his wife Ethel was at his side, just before midnight on June 3, 1968.

The tragedy of Vietnam affected the president
in many ways, and it overshadowed an agenda
that brought many benefits to the country.

When LBJ took office, only 8 percent of
Americans held college degrees. LBJ opened
college to many more Americans by his higher
education legislation, with grants, scholar-
ships, and work-study programs. Students have
received over 360 billion dollars through
financial aid under his Great Society
initiatives, and by the end of 2006, 21 percent
of US citizens held college diplomas.

LBJ got the Elementary and Secondary Education
Act through Congress. He recognized the need
for bilingual education for immigrants, and his
special education law has helped millions of
children with learning challenges.

He put civil rights and social justice before
the nation as moral issues. Under his
administration, the food stamp program and the
school breakfast program were created. He
signed into law the Medicare and Medicaid act,
providing over 100 million older citizens with
Medicare and millions of citizens at the
poverty level with Medicaid. Medicaid has been
the key factor in reducing infant deaths by
over 75 percent.

Under his administration, heart, cancer, and
stroke legislation provided funds to create
excellent medical facilities.

As a young man he was a schoolteacher in
Cotulla, Texas, a community of poor Hispanics.
He taught students who were too poor to wear
decent, clean clothing to school, to have
breakfast, or to make it to 12th grade and
graduate with a high school diploma. He once
told Congress: "It never occurred to me in my
fondest dreams that I might have the chance to
help the sons and daughters of those students
and to help people like them all over the
country. But now that I do have that chance—and
I'll let you in on a secret—I mean to use it."

There followed a legion of Great Society laws:

the Clean Air, Water Quality and Clean Water
Restoration Acts and Amendments.
The 1965 Solid Waste Disposal Act
The 1965 Motor Vehicle Air Pollution Control
Act, and the 1968 Aircraft Noises Abatement
Act. And later the Environmental Protection
Agency. . The Urban Mass Transit Act, and on and on

Johnson created 35 national parks. The 1968
Wild and Scenic Rivers Act that protects 165
river segments in 38 states and Puerto Rico.
The 1968 National Trail System has established
more than 1,000 trails covering close to 55,000
miles.

"Lyndon Johnson is our
greatest conservation president"

-National Geographic

Great Society initiatives include the
Kennedy Center for the Performing Arts
and the Hirshhorn Museum and Sculpture
Garden.

Johnson fulfilled a dream when he asked
Congress to establish the National Endowments
for the Arts and Humanities to provide
federal support for the arts and research.

If you watched Sesame Street, you can thank
LBJ. He established the Corporation for
Public Broadcasting, thus creating public
Radio and television.

Johnson created the Department of Transportation
and protected motorists by initiating
legislation that specifically covered auto
and tire safety. More products available to
consumers were covered by the Product Safety
Commission.

Historian David McCullough has said that the
threshold test of greatness in a President is
whether he is willing to risk his Presidency
for what he believes. LBJ passes that test
with flying colors.

LBJ and Congress enacted all this legislation in the 1960s:

1963
1. College Facilities
2. Clean Air
3. Vocational Education
4. Indian (Native American) Vocational Training
5. Manpower Training

1964
1. Inter-American Development Bank
2. Kennedy Cultural Center
3. Tax Reduction
4. Farm Program
5. Pesticide Controls
6. International Development Association
7. Civil Rights Act of 1964
8. Water Resources Research
9. War on Poverty
10. Criminal Justice
11. Truth-in-Securities
12. Food Stamps
13. Housing Act
14. Wilderness Areas
15. Nurse Training
16. Library Services

1965
1. Medicare
2. Medicaid
3. Elementary and Secondary Education
4. Higher Education
5. Bilingual Education
6. Department of Housing and Urban Development
7. Housing Act
8. Voting Rights
9. Immigration Reform Law
10. Older Americans
11. Heart, Cancer, Stroke Program
12. Law Enforcement Assistance
13. Drug Controls
14. Mental Health Facilities
15. Health Professions
16. Medical Libraries
17. Vocational Rehabilitation
18. Anti-Poverty Program
19. Arts and Humanities Foundation
20. Aid to Appalachia
21. Highway Beauty
22. Clean Air
23. Water Pollution Control
24. High Speed Transit
25. Manpower Training

> This list taken from a speech titled "Seeing Is Believing" by Joseph Califano Jr, on the LBJ Presidential Library website.

1965 con't

26. Child Health
27. Community Health Services
28. Water Resources Council
29. Water Desalting
30. Juvenile Delinquency Control
31. Arms Control
32. Affirmative Action

1966

1. Child Nutrition
2. Dept. of Transportation
3. Truth in Packaging
4. Model Cities
5. Rent Supplements
6. Teachers Corp
7. Asian Development Bank
8. Clean Rivers
9. Food for Freedom
10. Child Safety
11. Narcotics Rehabilitation
12. Traffic Safety
13. Highway Safety
14. Mine Safety
15. International Education
16. Bail Reform
17. Auto Safety
18. Tire Safety
19. New G.I. Bill
20. Minimum Wage Increase
21. Urban Mass Transit
22. Civil Procedure Reform
23. Fish and Wildlife Preservation
24. Water for Peace
25. Anti-Inflation Program
26. Scientific Knowledge Exchange
27. Protection for Savings
28. Freedom of Information
29. Hirshhorn Museum

1967

1. Education Professions
2. Education Act
3. Air Pollution Control
4. Partnership for Health
5. Social Security Increases
6. Age Discrimination

1967 (con't)

7. Wholesome Meat
8. Flammable Fabrics
9. Urban Research
10. Public Broadcasting
11. Modern DC Government
12. Outer Space Treaty
13. Federal Judicial Center
14. Deaf-Blind Center
15. College Work-Study
16. Summer Youth Programs
17. Food Stamps
18. Urban Fellowships
19. Safety at Sea Treaty
20. Narcotics Treaty
21. Anti-Racketeering
22. Product Safety Commission
23. Inter-American Bank

1968

1. Fair Housing
2. Indian Bill of Rights
3. Safe Streets
4. Wholesome Poultry
5. Commodity Exchange Rules
6. School Breakfasts
7. Truth-in-Lending
8. Aircraft Noise Abatement
9. New Narcotics Bureau
10. Gas Pipeline Safety
11. Fire Safety
12. Sea Grant Colleges
13. Tax Surcharge
14. Fair Housing Act
15. International Monetary Reform
16. Fair Federal Juries
17. Juvenile Delinquency Prevention
18. Guaranteed Student Loans
19. Health Manpower
20. Gun Control
21. Aid to Handicapped Children
22. Heart, Cancer, and Stroke Programs
23. Hazardous Radiation Protection
24. Scenic Rivers
25. Scenic Trails
26. National Water Commission
27. Vocational Education
28. Dangerous Drug Control
29. Military Justice Code
30. Tax Surcharge

—From From the LBJ
Library Website

Amor

Peace ♥ love

In April of 1967 Mrs. Johnson received a letter
from Jane Bokus asking Mrs. Johnson for her favorite
prayer. Mrs. Johnson had her social secretary Bess
Abell reply to the request. Ms. Abell replied,
"Although it would be most difficult for Mrs. Johnson
to choose one prayer as her favorite, we hope that this
verse, which holds special meaning for her, will be
suitable for your purpose."

"In the summer of 1962," Mrs. Johnson said,
"sitting on a wagon on a hillside in northern Greece,
a group of farmboys sang their prayer. I shall never
forget it—not only because of the setting and the
words, but because of the American Farm School in that
remote part of an American missionary. The words of the
song say just how much his footprints have meant."

A SONG OF PEACE

This is my song, O God of all the nations.
A song of peace for lands afar, and mine
This is my home, the country where my heart is,
This is my hope, my dream, my shrine:
But other hearts in other lands are beating
With hopes and dreams the same as mine.

My country's skies are bluer than the ocean
And sunlight beams on clover leaf and pine
But other lands have sunlight too, and clover,
And skies are sometimes blue as mine
Oh, hear my song, thou God of all the nations,
A song of peace for their land, and mine.

Mrs. Johnson sends her best wishes.

Sincerely,

Bess Abell
Social Secretary

Peace

Joy

Mrs. Johnson got lots of letters asking about a Texas
BBQ.... what did she serve??? I have copied a letter
below. This is a typical response from Lady Bird, gracious.

May 31, 1967

Dear Mr. Pollard and Mr. Roman:

        Mrs. Johnson asked me to Thank You for the
nice letter to the President.

        She was pleased to know of your interest in
learning what is served with beef at the Ranch. And we
are happy to list below a typical menu served on these
occasions:

Barbecued Beef and Ribs   Texas Cole Slaw
Chicken   Dill Pickles
Hot Link Sausage   Sliced Onions
Ranch Style Beans   Fried Apple Pies
German Potato Salad   Iced Tea
Sour Dough Biscuits   Coffee

Mrs. Johnson sends her best wishes for the success
of your party.

                              Sincerely,

                              Bess Abell
                              Social Secretary

Mr. James E. Pollock
Mr. Eddie Roman
Merrill Hills Country Club
Merrill Hills Road
Waukesha, Wisconsin

123

"HIM & HER"

Him and Her, the most well known of President Johnson's dogs, were registered beagles born on June 27, 1963.

In 1964, President Johnson raised the ire of many when he lifted Him by his ears while greeting a group on the WhiteHouse lawn. Johnson said he was just trying to get a good pose for a photograph.

"Him" died in June 1966; he was hit by a car while chasing a squirrel on the White House Lawn.

"Her" died at the White House after she swallowed a stone. Neither lived very long; the stone incident happened in 1964.

Him sired a litter of puppies born in October 1965. President Johnson's daughter, Luci, kept two of the puppies, Kim and Freckles. Kim moved to Texas with Luci after she married. Freckles stayed with the President at the White House. Smart dog!

☆ — LBJ Pets —

J. Edgar Hoover, director of the FBI gave
President Johnson another beagle after "Him"
died. President Johnson named the dog J. Edgar
but shortened it to Edgar. When Johnson left the
White House for his Texas Ranch Edgar moved with
the President and Lady Bird.

"J. Edgar"

☆ Blanco was a white collie given to the Johnsons
at the White House. He was a gift from a nine-year-
old girl from Illinois.

 Before moving back to Texas, Johnson gave Blanco
To a doctor and his wife who lived in Kentucky.

"Blanco"

"Dog is man's best friend!"
-Frederick the Great!

Perro/Hund
dog/chien

"Yuki"

President Lyndon Johnson's favorite dog was
a terrier mix named Yuki. Luci (daughter) found the
pup at a gas station in Texas on Thanksgiving Day
in 1966. LBJ took Yuki to cabinet meetings & the oval
office. Yuki enjoyed "singing" with the President.
"He is the friendliest and the smartest and the most
constant in his attentions of all the dogs that I've
known". - LBJ

"Ring buzz"

Fresca was LBJ's favorite (daytime) drink, according to historian Doris Kearns Goodwin. He had a special button installed on his desk in the Oval Office; when he pressed it, a military aide would appear with a cold one.

"No president except Jefferson relished a greater
variety of flavors in cookery than Lyndon B. Johnson.
He liked every style of cooking, and there was a saying
in the White House kitchen that LBJ would eat anything
that doesn't bite him first....He was partial to German
food, southern-style cooking, and French haute cuisine,
but his greatest love was Mexican foods."
—Francois Rysavy, A Treasury of White House Cooking

Zephyr Wright, the Johnson's longtime personal
cook, usually cooked what LBJ wanted, but when it came
to his diet, the president joked that Mrs. Wright was
boss. He didn't always accept her dictums without
grumbling, however. One evening, after complaints that
some of his favorite foods were being denied to him,
Johnson found this note from Zephyr under his plate:

Mr. President, you have been my boss for a number
of years and you always tell me you want to lose
weight, and yet you never do very much to help
yourself. Now I am going to be your boss for a
change. Eat what I put in front of you, and don't
ask for any more or complain.

The next night, the Johnsons were hosting a
diplomatic reception. In a conversation with Senator
William Fulbright, who had expressed the fear that "we
are succumbing to the arrogance of power," the
president denied Fulbright's assertion.
"A man can hardly have an arrogance of power when
he gets a note from his cook, talking up to him like
this." And he pulls Zephyr's note from his pocket and
reads it aloud. "If and when I feel arrogance of power,
Zephyr will take it out on me."

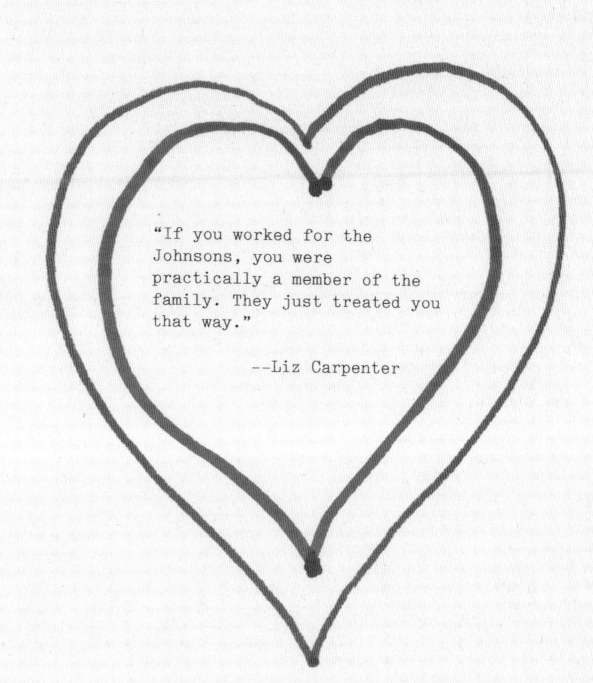

"If you worked for the Johnsons, you were practically a member of the family. They just treated you that way."

--Liz Carpenter

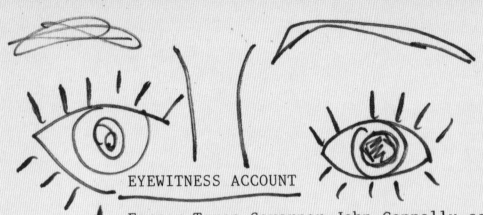

EYEWITNESS ACCOUNT

Former Texas Governor John Connally said this about
LBJ.
"Most of the time he had no manners. He'd eat off the
plate of either person on either side of him. If he
ate something that he liked and they hadn't finished
theirs, he'd reach over with his fork and eat off of
their plate."

Spies tell us that President Johnson was a nibbler.
At receptions and cocktail parties, he had been known
to stand before a bowl of deep- fried shrimp and
demolish them practically single-handed.

While I should point out that I could not confirm the
following, it's said that LBJ ate at least one hot dog
per inning while watching a baseball game. That's a lot
of hot dogs!

I read the book Lyndon: An Oral Biography by Merle Miller,
and found lots of LBJ eating-off-other-plates stories. The
following was told by George Christian:
"LBJ would be talking, and maybe he'd reach over and get
somebody else's butter. I remember on the press plane coming
back from Australia to Manila for the Manila Conference in
1966, the Prime Minister of New Zealand and his wife flew with
him up there...And they were all having breakfast in the cabin
of the plane with some of the press around, and he just absent-
mindedly reached over and ate a piece of bacon off the plate
of the Prime Minister's wife. The press got hold of it and
blew it up, almost made an international incident out of it."

Mr. Christian goes on to say, "It was just him. If somebody
would be sitting on his right and eating ice cream--he was
on his diet half the time and craved sweets--all of a sudden
he'd just reach over and take a spoonful of ice cream. Like
some kid."

EYEWITNESS ACCOUNT, con't.

  ... Several times he told me, 'I'm cooped up in this place, and
I don't have a minute of my own. I'm beset with problems. They
don't bring me anything unless it can go either way, and I have
to decide it.' And he said, 'By GOD I'm going to do what I want
to do. If I want to drink a scotch whiskey. And if I want to have
bad manners, I'm going to have bad manners. I'm going to have
some freedom to do what I want to do.'

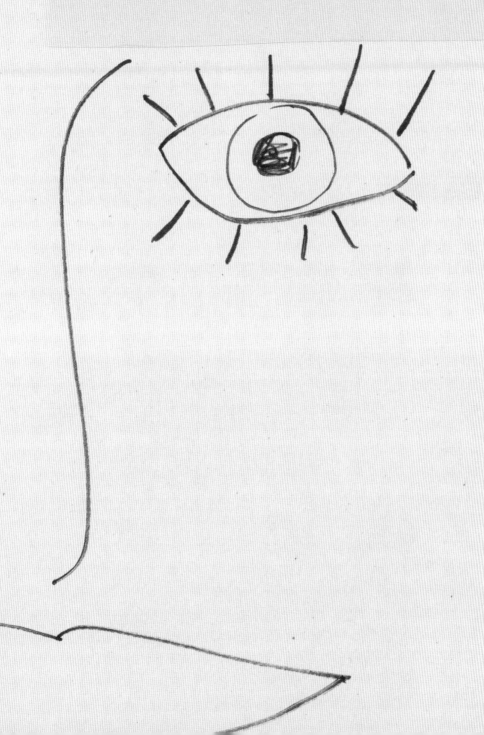

Weddings in the White
HOUSE

The President and Mrs. Johnson's years in the
White House were marked by two single personal
events, the weddings of their daughters Luci Baines
and Lynda Bird.
When Lynda Bird Johnson married Charles S. Robb, on
December 9, 1967, it was the first wedding of a
President's daughter in the White House since Eleanor
Randolph, Woodrow Wilson's daughter, married William
McAdoo in 1914. The ceremony was private and was
held in the East Room.

        As with Luci's wedding, Lynda Bird's reception
featured an elaborate buffet. The hot dishes included
lobster barquettes, crabmeat bouchees, stuffed mushrooms, miniature shishkebab, and Quiche Lorraine.
Among cold platters were, sliced smoked salmon with
capers, molds of chicken liver pate, iced shrimp, and
assorted cheeses and finger sandwiches.
The bride chose an old-fashioned pound cake for the
five-layer wedding cake. It was iced with a white fondant
and decorated with sugar scrolls, loops and braids, pulled
-sugar roses, and white lovebirds, and topped with a sugar
basket of real white roses.

        Both girls entertained their bridesmaids at the
White House and gave them mementos of the occasion.
Their menus may have varied, but both girls
concluded with a dessert of Flowerpot Sundaes.

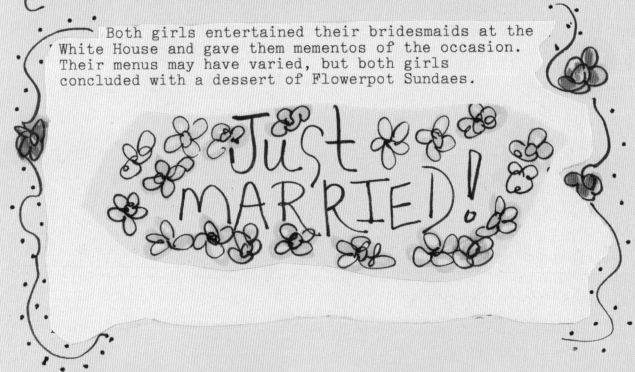

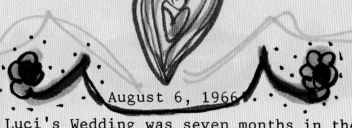

August 6, 1966

Luci's Wedding was seven months in the planning.
55 million people watched it on TV.
19 year old Luci married Pat Nugent at the Shrine
of the Immaculate Conception in front of 700 guests.

The secret of where the couple was going on
their honeymoon lasted one day. Traveling as
Mr. and Mrs. Frisbee, they turned up in the
Bahamas where they relaxed in a 10 room villa
outside of Nassau.

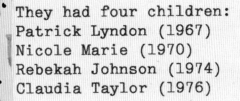

They had four children:
Patrick Lyndon (1967)
Nicole Marie (1970)
Rebekah Johnson (1974)
Claudia Taylor (1976)

Luci and Pat later divorced, and the marriage
was annulled by the Catholic Church in August 1979.

On March 3, 1984, she married Ian J. Turpin (born 1944)
Luci has one step-son. Mr. Turpin is an Anglican.

NOTE: During my research at the LBJ Library I
  discovered that a very small sliver of wedding cake
    is in the file. It looked like sawdust to me.

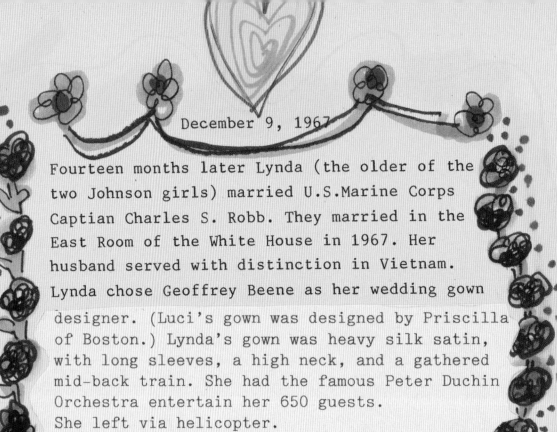

December 9, 1967

Fourteen months later Lynda (the older of the
two Johnson girls) married U.S.Marine Corps
Captian Charles S. Robb. They married in the
East Room of the White House in 1967. Her
husband served with distinction in Vietnam.
Lynda chose Geoffrey Beene as her wedding gown
designer. (Luci's gown was designed by Priscilla
of Boston.) Lynda's gown was heavy silk satin,
with long sleeves, a high neck, and a gathered
mid-back train. She had the famous Peter Duchin
Orchestra entertain her 650 guests.
She left via helicopter.

Lynda and Charles Robb have three daughters.
Lucinda Desha Robb (born 1968)
Catherine Lewis Robb (born 1970)
Jennifer Wickliffe Robb (born 1978)

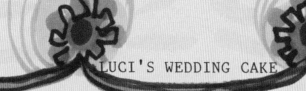

LUCI'S WEDDING CAKE

1 3/4 cups sifted cake flour
1 teaspoon double acting
  baking powder
1/4 teaspoon salt
1/2 cup butter
3/4 cup sugar
1/2 teaspoon vanilla extract

5 egg whites, unbeaten
3/4 cup chopped candied
  pineapple
1 cup chopped pecans
1/2 cup soaked raisins
1/2 teaspoon almond
  extract

Cover 1/2 cup white seedless raisins with apple juice and let soak in refrigerator two or three days (or until raisins are plump). Drain and spread on paper towel to dry/ absorb moisture.

Sift flour once and measure. Add baking powder and salt and sift together three times.
Cream butter throughly and gradually add sugar, creaming together until light and fluffy.
Add egg whites one at a time, beating throughly after each. Add fruit nuts and flavoring and mix well. Add flour, a little at a time, beating after each addition until smooth.

Bake in an 8" X 8" X 3" pan that has been greased, lined with heavy paper, and greased again. Bake in a 300F oven about one hour and fifteen minutes, or until a toothpick inserted in center comes out clean. Frost as desired. Serves eight to ten.

the cake was decorated with delicate archways and 60 handmade flowers made from sugar. The seven-layer cake weighed about 300 lbs.!
-aug. 6, 1966

"Mrs. Johnson and the President I think
never wanted to shelter their children
from public life. There are many people in
the political arena who want to keep their
children away from it, not let it touch them.
But the President and Mrs. Johnson felt that
there were so many benefits that would come
to them that they wanted to involve them in
everything from campaigning to official
trips abroad with their parents and State
Dinners at the White House.

Mrs. Johnson would from time to time ask one
of the girls to stand in for her to receive a
group at a tea or coffee. She always wanted them
to come to the State dinners when they were in
town.

She would also tell them when she invited them
that if we ended up with too many guests they'd
have to eat in the Navy Mess with the staff,
and they were both good sports about it. They'd

put on their best dress and go and greet and meet
and have a marvelous time with the guests during
cocktail hour; then the guests would go into the
dinner and the girls would join the military social

aides and me and go over and have dinner in the
Navy Mess and then make a beeline back and then
greet some of the guests who were coming in at
ten o'clock for the entertainment."

--Bess Abell, Social Secretary
oral history file--II-7

Advice Lady Bird gave her daughters and still
wise words.

"Don't do anything you wouldn't mind seeing
on the front of the newspapers."

                            -Lady Bird

Lady Bird always said:

"An election is won or lost in the last week"

                            -Lady Bird

"And another thing that Mrs. Johnson always
    felt, a room isn't a room if it has more than one
                        door."

                        --Bess Abell, social
                                    secretary

Meats and Poultry

MARINATED SZECHWAN CHICKEN SALAD

SALAD:

6 deboned chicken breasts, skin removed
1 large head Romaine lettuce, rinsed and patted dry

1 medium head of white cabbage, thinly sliced

2 large carrots, peeled and grated (1-1 1/2 cups)
6 scallions, finely chopped
Fresh fruit for garnish

Dressing:

5 large fresh basil leaves
1/8 teaspoon red chili flakes
1 teaspoon Szechwan peppercorns
1/4 cup grated fresh ginger root
1 clove garlic, crushed
2 tablespoons honey
1/4 cup soy sauce
1/4 cup red wine vinegar
1/4 cup toasted sesame oil
1/2 cup water

Combine dressing ingredients in a blender or food processor. Process until smooth.

Reserve 3/4 cup for the dressing

Marinate the chicken breasts in the remaining dressing for at least one hour. Preheat oven to 350F. Grill chicken breasts on each side for 2 mins. Place in large baking pan and bake until cooked, about 12 minutes. Cool and slice into strips.

Arrange lettuce leaves, cabbage, carrots and scallions on six chilled plates. Place about 4 or 5 chicken strips over the lettuce.
Spoon 2 tablespoons of the dressing over salad.
Garnish with fresh fruit.

Makes 6 servings.

I'm chicken

I'm so.... cute!

..why eat me?

WHOLE ROAST BEEF TENDERLOIN
OR BEEF BORDELAISE

Preheat oven to 450F.

Trim and tie the tenderloin and place in a
heavy pan. On the stove top, quickly sear in
a small amount of fat, turning until all sides
are browned.

When tenderloin is browned, place it in the oven. Roast for 5
minutes, then reduce heat to 375F and continue baking for 10 to
15 minutes longer, depending on how well done you like the meat.

Remove the tenderloin from the pan and place on rack in
a warm place with air circulation. Allow to rest for 15 to 20
minutes, then transfer to a cutting board and slice. Serve
immediately with Bordelaise sauce.

Bordelaise Sauce

In a heavy saucepan melt 1/2 cup butter. Add one chopped carrot
and two medium chopped onions. Cook until golden brown, stirring
often.

Add one-half cup flour and cook, stirring frequently,
until the roux takes on a good hazelnut brown color
and the carrot and onions are brown. Bring to a boil.
Add three cups hot beef stock, one clove garlic, a
bouquet garni made by tying together one stalk celery,
three or 4 sprigs parsley, a small bay leaf, and a pinch
of thyme. Cook, stirring frequently, until thickened and
add three more cups of hot beef stock. Cook the sauce
very slowly over low heat, stirring occasionally, for one
hour, or until reduced to three cups.

Add one-fourth cup tomato sauce or half cup tomato puree.
Cook the sauce a few minutes longer. Remove the bouquet
garni and strain the sauce through a fine sieve. Add two
more cups of hot stock and cook the sauce slowly for about
one hour more, or until reduced to about four cups, Cool.
Serve with Beef Bordelaise or freeze in small containers.

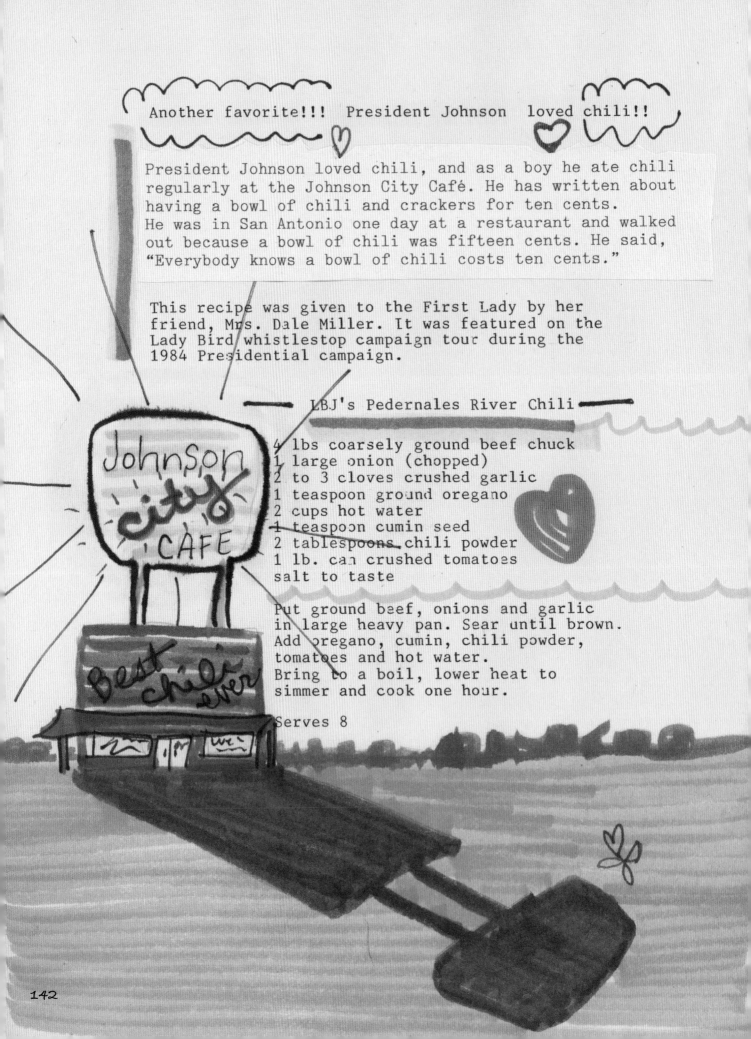

Another favorite!!! President Johnson loved chili!!

President Johnson loved chili, and as a boy he ate chili
regularly at the Johnson City Café. He has written about
having a bowl of chili and crackers for ten cents.
He was in San Antonio one day at a restaurant and walked
out because a bowl of chili was fifteen cents. He said,
"Everybody knows a bowl of chili costs ten cents."

This recipe was given to the First Lady by her
friend, Mrs. Dale Miller. It was featured on the
Lady Bird whistlestop campaign tour during the
1984 Presidential campaign.

LBJ's Pedernales River Chili

4 lbs coarsely ground beef chuck
1 large onion (chopped)
2 to 3 cloves crushed garlic
1 teaspoon ground oregano
2 cups hot water
1 teaspoon cumin seed
2 tablespoons chili powder
1 lb. can crushed tomatoes
salt to taste

Put ground beef, onions and garlic
in large heavy pan. Sear until brown.
Add oregano, cumin, chili powder,
tomatoes and hot water.
Bring to a boil, lower heat to
simmer and cook one hour.

Serves 8

Johnson City CAFE

Best chili ever

142

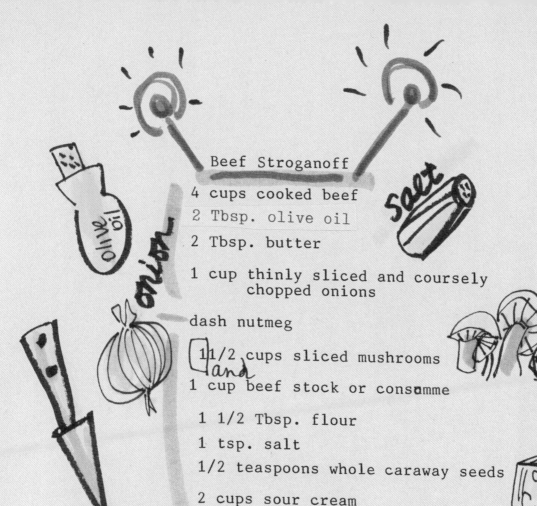

Beef Stroganoff

4 cups cooked beef

2 Tbsp. olive oil

2 Tbsp. butter

1 cup thinly sliced and coursely
    chopped onions

dash nutmeg

1 1/2 cups sliced mushrooms
and
1 cup beef stock or consomme

1 1/2 Tbsp. flour

1 tsp. salt

1/2 teaspoons whole caraway seeds

2 cups sour cream

Trim all fat from the meat and cut in strips
about 1/2" wide. Heat oil and butter in
skillet; add onions and mushrooms and saute
at low heat until soft.
Add meat and continue cooking for 10 minutes.
Add consomme and cook for 30 minutes.
Mix flour and seasonings with the sour cream
and add to first mixture.
Cook slowly until thick, but do not boil.
Remove from direct heat and keep over hot
water.

Serve with rice or thin noodles.

butter, onion
oil, mushroom

ADD MEAT

seasonings,
mix flour, sour
creme

mix

Serve with rice or — thin noodles.

POT ROAST

2 tablespoons honey

1 tablespoon A-1 sauce
or Worchestershire

1 lean pot roast, boned
and rolled

1/4 teaspoon marjoram

1 teaspoon salt

1 cup water

2 onions, sliced

2 stalks celery,
chopped

1/2 teaspoon salt

Trim fat from roast and roll. Heat honey and A-1 or
Worchestershire in bottom of a heavy kettle over
moderate heat. Add pot roast, turning to coat evenly.
Brown. Add rest of ingredients. Cover and cook for
3-4 hours until meat is tender. Add water if necessary.

BAAAA — BROILED LAMB PATTIES

1 pound lean ground lamb

1 cup grated raw carrot

1 egg, slightly beaten

1/4 teaspoon pepper

1/4 teaspoon curry
powder

2 tablespoons minced
onion

1 teaspoon salt

Combine ingredients and mix well. Shape into 6
patties. Broil 5 minutes on each side 4 inches
from heat.

Note to
self:

Wine, cheese and lamb.
Shown to stave off dementia.

EMPANADAS

Meat filling (recipe below)
4 1/2 cups sifted all-purpose flour
4 1/2 teaspoons baking powder
2 1/4 teaspoons salt
1 1/4 cups soft shortening
2/3 cup cold water

Prepare meat filling and let cool while
making pastry. Sift flour, baking powder and
salt into a bowl. Addshortening and cut
in with two knives or pastry blender until
mixture resembles coarse corn meal. Sprinkle
water, one tablespoon at a time over flour
mixture, tossing with a fork until mixture
clings together. Roll out dough 1/8 inch
thick on a lightly floured board. Cut into
rounds with a 3 1/4 inch cookie cutter or
a 5 ounce custard cup. Heat oven to 400F.
Spoon a heaping teaspoon of meat mixture
onto one side of each round. Wet edge of
pastry and fold in half; press edges together
with fork to seal in filling. Prick top
of pastry with tines of fork. Arrange on
greased cookie sheet and bake 15 to 20 mins,
until golden brown.   Makes about 4 1/2dozen.

MEAT FILLING

1/2 pound ground pork
1/2 pound ground beef
1/2 cup seedless raisins
1/2 cup thinly sliced stuffed green olives
1/4 cup tomato paste
1/2 teaspoon Worcestershire sauce
1/4 cup drained capers
Dash of Tabasco
1/2 teaspoon salt
1/4 teaspoon ground pepper

Cook meats in a skillet over low heat
for ten minutes, or until no longer
pink.
Drain off excess fat and mix with remaining
ingredients.

TEXAS FRIED CHICKEN

Chicken (3 pound)   2 cups finely ground cracker crumbs
1 tablespoon salt   Butter or Lard
1 tablespoon pepper   1/2 cup flour
1 egg   1/4 cup milk
1/4 cup chicken stock

Clean chicken and cut into pieces. Pat dry chicken and
sprinkle with flour mixture (flour, salt, pepper).
Take one piece of chicken and dip into a mixture of
one egg and 1/4 cup milk that has been mixed together.
Then dip into ground cracker crumbs and place in a hot
skillet in which lard or butter has melted. Repeat with all.

Brown all the pieces.
Add 1/4 cup boiling hot chicken stock to the pan of chicken.
Cover the pan and place in hot oven (300 degrees) and cook
about half hour or until tender.
If you prefer a thicker sauce, add a little flour to thicken
the drippings. Serve hot or cold. Serves 4

3 winners

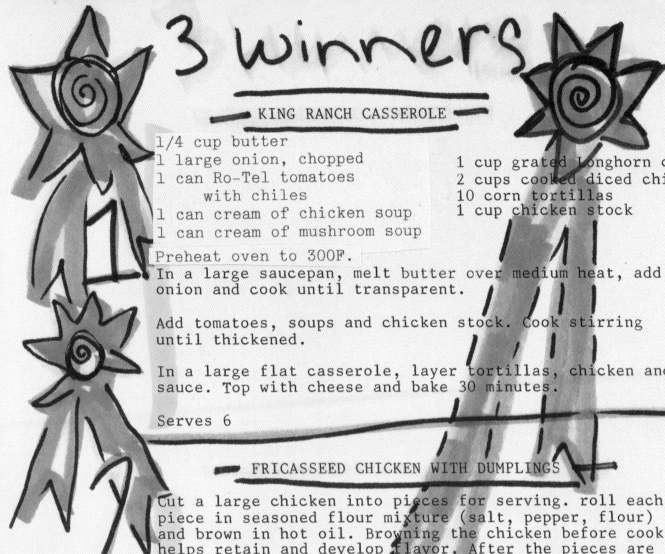

KING RANCH CASSEROLE

1/4 cup butter
1 large onion, chopped
1 can Ro-Tel tomatoes
    with chiles
1 can cream of chicken soup
1 can cream of mushroom soup

1 cup grated Longhorn cheese
2 cups cooked diced chicken
10 corn tortillas
1 cup chicken stock

Preheat oven to 300F.

In a large saucepan, melt butter over medium heat, add
onion and cook until transparent.

Add tomatoes, soups and chicken stock. Cook stirring
until thickened.

In a large flat casserole, layer tortillas, chicken and
sauce. Top with cheese and bake 30 minutes.

Serves 6

FRICASSEED CHICKEN WITH DUMPLINGS

Cut a large chicken into pieces for serving. roll each
piece in seasoned flour mixture (salt, pepper, flour)
and brown in hot oil. Browning the chicken before cooking
helps retain and develop flavor. After the pieces are
browned, simmer until tender in enough water to cover.
When it is done, take the chicken out and cook dumplings
in the gravy. Serve the chicken in the center of a platter
with the dumplings around the edge. Pour the gravy over
the chicken.

DUMPLINGS

1 cup flour

1/2 teaspoon salt

1/3 cup whole milk

2 1/2 teaspoons baking
                powder
1 egg

Sift the flour, baking powder, and salt together. Beat
the egg well; add the milk, and mix in the dry ingredients.
Drop batter by small spoonsful into the chicken gravy.
Cover tightly and cook for 15 minutes. The lid must not be
lifted while the dumplings are cooking. If the steam escapes,
the dumplings will not get light and fluffy.

147

Beef King Ranch Casserole

2 pounds beef sirloin
1 cup onion, chopped
1/2 cup red bell pepper, chopped
1/2 cup green bell pepper, chopped
2 to 4 tablespoons jalapeños, chopped
1 teaspoon salt
1 teaspoon pepper
1 teaspoon cumin
1 teaspoon garlic powder
1 tablespoon chili powder
2/3 cup skim milk
10-ounce can diced green chiles and tomatoes
16-ounce can beef broth
8 ounces cheddar cheese, shredded
12 corn tortillas

Cook beef over low heat with water until fork tender; 30 to 45 minutes.

Place cooked meat on a hard surface and shred by pulling apart with two forks. Set aside.
Prepare a large skillet with non-stick cooking spray.
Saute onion and peppers with dry ingredients until translucent.
Add chiles and tomatoes, beef broth, and milk. Simmer. Stir in cheese until melted.
Add cooked shredded meat.
Quarter tortillas and add to mixture.
Pour into casserole dish prepared with nonstick cooking spray. Bake at 350F for 30 minutes. Serves 8.

148

ROAST LONG ISLAND DUCKLING WITH APRICOTS

1 5-pound duckling
1 tablespoon butter or margarine
1 tablespoon flour
1 cup very hot water
1/2 cup dry white wine
2 small oranges
1 16-ounce can apricot halves
1 1/2 teaspoons flour
1 tablespoon dark brown sugar
1/4 cup dry white wine
1/2 teaspoon salt

Heat oven to 450. Wash and dry duck. Sprinkle inside of duck with salt.
Place in roasting pan and roast 20 mins., or until lightly browned. Remove duck from oven and reduce oven temperature to 350.
Remove duck from pan and drain off fat. Pour 1 tablespoon of the fat back into pan; add butter and heat until butter is melted. Blend in 1 tablespoon flour and cook over low heat until lightly browned. Gradually add hot water and the 1/2 cup wine; cook over low heat until sauce is thickened. Return duck to sauce in pan and roast 1 1/2 hours, basting occasionally, or until thigh joint moves freely. While duck is roasting, peel oranges, using only yellow outside of skin. Cut into very thin, long strips; place in boiling water and cook 2 minutes. Remove from heat and strain, reserving peel.

Remove white membrane from oranges and cut oranges into sections to use for garnish.
At the end of roasting time, remove duck from pan and drain all juices and fat. Skim off all the fat. Drain apricots and reserve juice. Spoon 1 1/2 tablespoons of fat back into the pan; add the 1 1/2 tablespoons flour and stir until blended. Cook over low heat; stirring constantly, until thickened. Add sugar, salt and orange peel; heat. Serve with duck. Garnish duck with orange sections and apricot halves. Serves 4

149

Seafood

You Need to Know:

1/2 fillet of wild salmon is ~ 281 calories
"   - farm raised is 412 calories.
Wild salmon - 13 grams fat
farm raised - 27 "   " . Stick with "Wild"

Buy 1 of these 6.
HERB FISH STEAKS

4 salmon, haddock, or halibut steaks

1 cup white wine vinegar

2 bay leaves

1/2 teaspoon thyme

1 teaspoon minced onion

Combine and mix all ingredients but fish.

Pour into a shallow bowl. Add fish.

Let marinate 1/2- 3/4 hour.

Drain fish.

Coat liberally with olive oil.

Grease grill to prevent sticking.

Baste each side with marinade.

Grill on each side 5 minutes.

VARIETIES of Salmon

DOG SALMON

PINK SALMON

Atlantic Salmon

CHINOOK SALMON

COHO SALMON

Sockeye SALMON

Note:
Atlantic Salmon
Sold commercially
is prob. farm-
raised.

Lobster Barquettes

1 tablespoon finely chopped shallots

2 tablespoon butter

2 cups diced cooked lobster meat

1/2 cup heavy cream

1 cup whipped cream

1 cup Hollandaise Sauce

pinch cayenne pepper

grated Parmesan cheese

24 barquettes (Oval pastry shells)

Saute shallots in butter until translucent. Add
Lobster meat and (unwhipped) cream.
Mix carefully and fill each barquette about 3/4 full.
Fold whipped cream into hollandaise. Add a pinch of
cayenne pepper. Spread over lobster mixture; dust
with grated cheese.
Place under broiler until sauce is bubbly and slightly
browned.
MAKES 24, A WONDERFUL APPETIZER

Hey.

yikes!
you are
eating
my friend!

Shrimp Curry a la Zephyr Wright

2 lbs. raw shrimp, shelled and deveined
5 tablespoons butter
1/2 cup minced onions
6 tablespoons flour
2 and 1/2 teaspoons curry powder

1 and 1/4 teaspoons salt
1 teaspoon sugar
1/2 teaspoon powdered ginger
1 chicken bouillon cube, dissolved in 1 cup boiling water
2 cups milk

1 teaspoon lemon juice

Steam shrimp until done- about 5 min or until pink.

Saute onions in melted butter until tender.

Stir in flour, curry powder, salt, sugar and ginger.

Dissolve bouillion cube in boiling water.

Gradually combine bouillon and milk with onion and spice mixture, stirring until thickened.

Add cooked shrimp and lemon juice, cooking until heated. *Serve over white rice.*

Makes 8 servings.

LADY BIRD'S SHRIMP SQUASH CASSEROLE

3 cups sliced yellow squash
3/4 cup raw shrimp (cleaned and deveined)
2 tablespoons butter
2 tablespoons flour
1/2 teaspoon salt
1/8 teaspoon black pepper
1 cup chicken broth
1/2 cup whipping cream (chilled)
1 tablespoon finely minced onion
1/2 cup coarse bread crumbs
1/4 cup grated parmesan cheese
1 tablespoon melted butter

Good Stuff!

Wash and dry squash. Cut crosswise into 1/4 inch slices.

Throughly rinse shrimp under cold water and drain.

Heat 2 tablespoons of butter in a sauce pan. Blend in

flour,salt and pepper. Cook until it bubbles.

Remove from heat and add chicken broth gradually,

stirring constantly. Bring to a boil for 1 or 2 minutes.

Blend in cream and minced onions. Mix in raw shrimp.

Layer squash in 1 1/2 quart casserole dish. Spoon half

of shrimp sauce over squash. Repeat with remaining squash

and shrimp sauce.

Cover tightly and place in a 400F oven for 30 minutes.

Meanwhile toss breadcrumbs and Parmesan cheese with

melted butter. After 30 minutes top squash/shrimp with

crumbs. Reduce oven heat to 350F and return casserole to

oven for 15 minutes or until crumbs are golden brown.

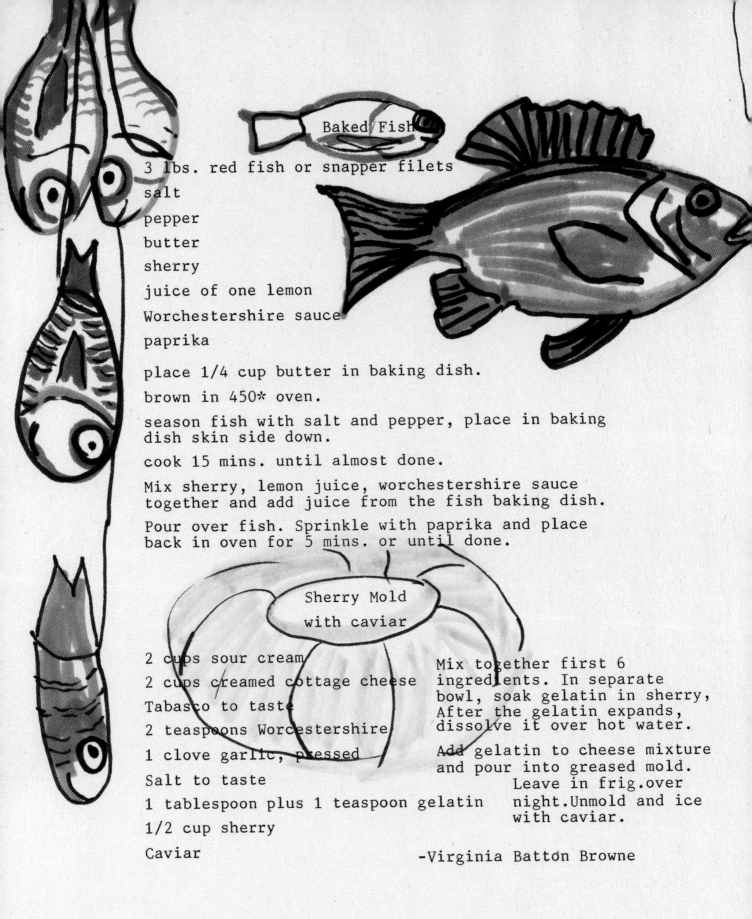

Baked Fish

3 lbs. red fish or snapper filets

salt

pepper

butter

sherry

juice of one lemon

Worchestershire sauce

paprika

place 1/4 cup butter in baking dish.

brown in 450* oven.

season fish with salt and pepper, place in baking dish skin side down.

cook 15 mins. until almost done.

Mix sherry, lemon juice, worchestershire sauce together and add juice from the fish baking dish.

Pour over fish. Sprinkle with paprika and place back in oven for 5 mins. or until done.

Sherry Mold with caviar

2 cups sour cream

2 cups creamed cottage cheese

Tabasco to taste

2 teaspoons Worcestershire

1 clove garlic, pressed

Salt to taste

1 tablespoon plus 1 teaspoon gelatin

1/2 cup sherry

Caviar

Mix together first 6 ingredients. In separate bowl, soak gelatin in sherry, After the gelatin expands, dissolve it over hot water.

Add gelatin to cheese mixture and pour into greased mold. Leave in frig. over night. Unmold and ice with caviar.

-Virginia Batton Browne

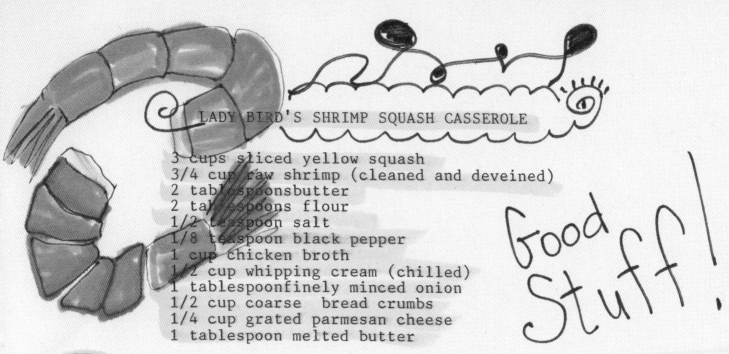

LADY BIRD'S SHRIMP SQUASH CASSEROLE

3 cups sliced yellow squash
3/4 cup raw shrimp (cleaned and deveined)
2 tablespoonsbutter
2 tablespoons flour
1/2 teaspoon salt
1/8 teaspoon black pepper
1 cup chicken broth
1/2 cup whipping cream (chilled)
1 tablespoonfinely minced onion
1/2 cup coarse bread crumbs
1/4 cup grated parmesan cheese
1 tablespoon melted butter

Good Stuff!

Wash and dry squash. Cut crosswise into 1/4 inch slices.

Throughly rinse shrimp under cold water and drain.

Heat 2 tablespoons of butter in a sauce pan. Blend in

flour,salt and pepper. Cook until it bubbles.

Remove from heat and add chicken broth gradually,

stirring constantly. Bring to a boil for 1 or 2 minutes.

Blend in cream and minced onions. Mix in raw shrimp.

Layer squash in 1 1/2 quart casserole dish. Spoon half

of shrimp sauce over squash. Repeat with remaining squash

and shrimp sauce.

Cover tightly and place in a 400F oven for 30 minutes.

Meanwhile toss crumbs and parmesan cheese with melted

margarune. After 30 minutes top squash/shrimp with bread

crumbs. Reduce oven heat to 350F and return casserole to

oven for 15 minutes or until crumbs are golden brown.

Sides

EGGPLANT

Eggplant Casserole

1 large eggplant	1 can tomatoes
1 can of tomato paste (6oz)	2 crushed garlic cloves
1 tsp. of salt	dash of pepper
1 can of mushrooms (3 oz.)	1/2 cup grated Parmesan
2 cups soft bread crumbs	1/2 lb. thinly sliced mozzarella

Cut eggplant into cubes. Saute in oil until tender;
reserve. Combine tomatoes, tomato paste, garlic, salt,
and pepper in a saucepan; simmer 15 minutes.

Stir in mushrooms, Parmesan cheese, and breadcrumbs.
Mix well and add eggplant. Heat thoroughly.

Heat oven to 375F. Spoon eggplant mixture into
casserole dish. Top with cheese slices. Bake
15 to 20 minutes, or until cheese is melted and
casserole is lightly browned.

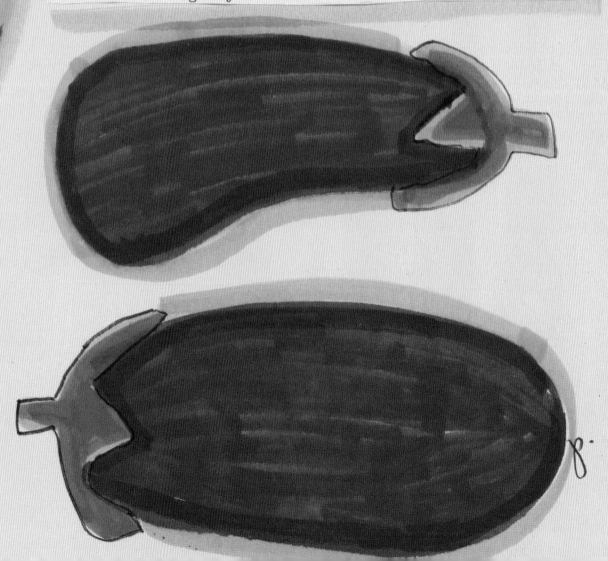

Eggplant Nicoise

- this was included on the menu for a State Dinner given in honor of the King and Queen of Thailand.

2 large eggplants
3 tablespoons vegtable oil
1 medium-sized onion, diced
2 garlic cloves, chopped
2 teaspoons salt
1/4 teaspoon freshly ground pepper
1 tablespoon chopped fresh parsley

6 drops of Tabasco sauce
4 tomatoes, peeled and seeded. Or one 14-ounce can whole tomatoes, drained.

1/2 cup bread crumbs

1/2 cup grated Parmesan cheese
pinch of paprika

Pre-heat oven to 350
Split eggplants in half lengthwise and gently scoop out the pulp without puncturing the skin; dice pulp.

Lightly brush insides of empty eggplant shells with oil and place in ungreased baking dish, cavities up. Bake for 10 minutes, or until slightly softened.
In a non-stick frying pan, heat remaining oil, add onion and garlic and saute until golden brown.
Add diced eggplant, salt, parsley, pepper, Tabasco sauce, and tomatoes; simmer for 10 minutes.
Combine the breadcrumbs and cheese and fold half into the eggplant mixture. Spoon evenly into the baked shells.
Sprinkle with the remaining crumb-cheese mixture and a dash of paprika.
Bake on middle shelf of a 375 oven for 20 to 25 minutes, or until golden brown. Serve at once.

Asian Long Eggplant

WESTERN EGGPLANT

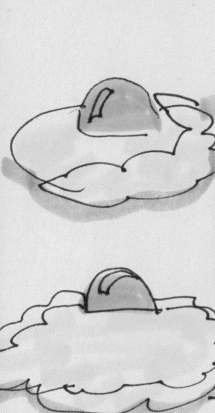

Quiche Andalouse

1 9" pie crust
2 medium eggplants
3 eggs
1 cup milk
1 cup heavy cream
½ tsp. salt
dash of nutmeg
dash of white pepper
1 small onion, minced
1 Tbsp. butter
1 cup grated Swiss cheese

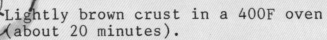

— Lightly brown crust in a 400F oven (about 20 minutes).
— Preheat oven to 350F. Peel and slice eggplants into 1/4" rounds. Toss with salt and let stand in a collander to drain 30 minutes.
— Blot dry with paper towels; dust with flour and deep fry in hot oil until golden. Drain on paper towel.

— Combine and beat lightly eggs, milk, heavy cream, salt, nutmeg, and white pepper.
— Saute onion in butter until tender.
— Cool and add to the egg mixture.

— Layer half of the eggplant slices over the crust. Cover with 1/2 cup Swiss Cheese, and a scoop of the egg mixture.
— Arrange another layer of eggplant on top and cover with the remaining egg mixture.
— Top with the remaining Swiss cheese.

— Bake at 350F for 40 minutes or until golden brown and puffed.

— Cool 10 minutes before serving.

— Serves 8 to 10

True grit is making a decision and standing by it, doing what must be done - John Wayne (Lady Bird liked him alot

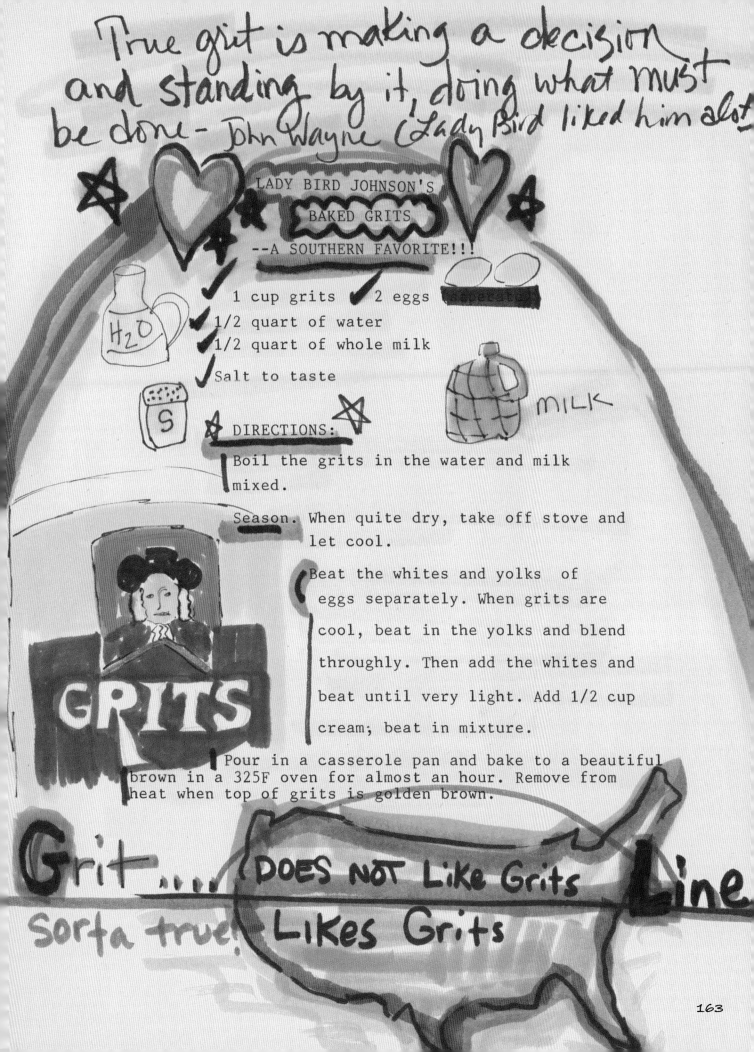

LADY BIRD JOHNSON'S BAKED GRITS

--A SOUTHERN FAVORITE!!!

1 cup grits   2 eggs seperated
1/2 quart of water
1/2 quart of whole milk
Salt to taste

DIRECTIONS:

Boil the grits in the water and milk mixed.

Season. When quite dry, take off stove and let cool.

Beat the whites and yolks of eggs separately. When grits are cool, beat in the yolks and blend throughly. Then add the whites and beat until very light. Add 1/2 cup cream; beat in mixture.

Pour in a casserole pan and bake to a beautiful brown in a 325F oven for almost an hour. Remove from heat when top of grits is golden brown.

Grit.....Line

DOES NOT LIKE Grits

LIKES Grits

Sorta true!

Life is good with cheese grits!

Longhorn

Hmm... looks like a purse. But it's a cheese grinder.

CHEESE GRITS......

Cook 1 cup grits in 4 cups boiling water, add 1 teaspoon on salt.

Cook over medium stovetop for 20 minutes. When grits are cooked add 2 cups of shredded cheese and one stick butter. Stir until butter is melted and cheese is blended in mixture.

Pour mixture in well-buttered casserole dish and bake for 1 hour at 325F.

Serves 4 to 6 people.

Happy Day! Baking cheese GRITS!

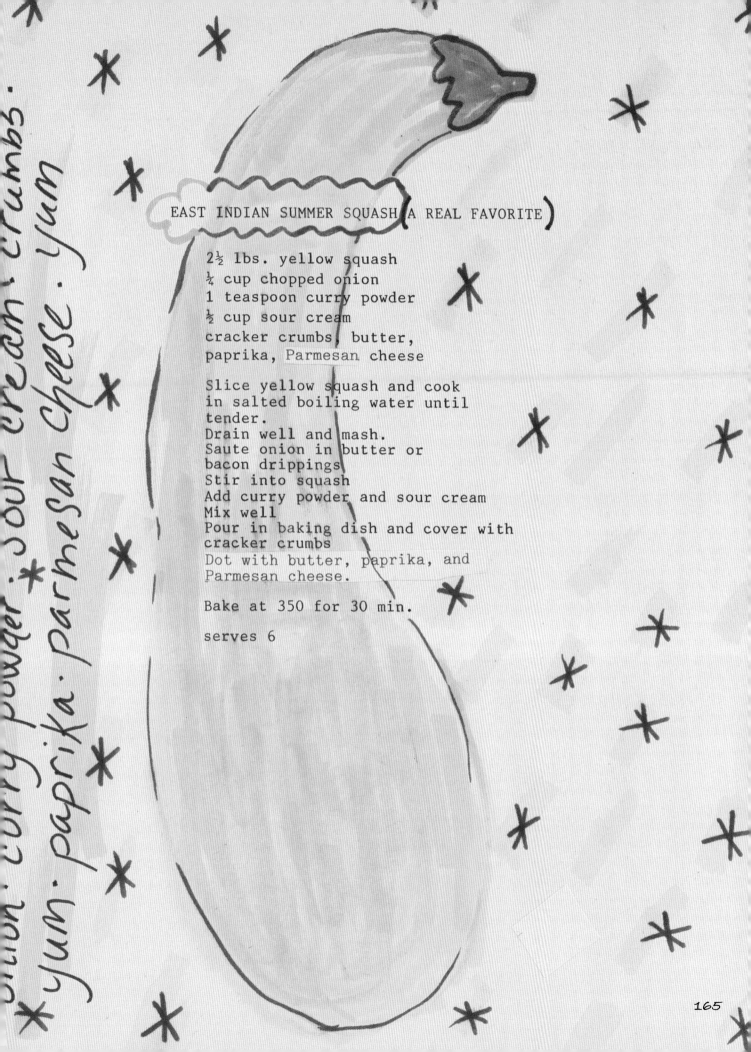

EAST INDIAN SUMMER SQUASH (A REAL FAVORITE)

2½ lbs. yellow squash
¼ cup chopped onion
1 teaspoon curry powder
½ cup sour cream
cracker crumbs, butter,
paprika, Parmesan cheese

Slice yellow squash and cook
in salted boiling water until
tender.
Drain well and mash.
Saute onion in butter or
bacon drippings
Stir into squash
Add curry powder and sour cream
Mix well
Pour in baking dish and cover with
cracker crumbs
Dot with butter, paprika, and
Parmesan cheese.

Bake at 350 for 30 min.

serves 6

Squash Casserole--

2 1/2 pounds squash (yellow and zucchini) sliced

4 eggs

1/2 cup milk

1 pound Monterey Jack cheese, cubed or grated

1 teaspoon salt

2 teaspoons baking powder

3 tablespoons flour

1/2 cup chopped parsley

4 4oz. cans chopped or sliced green chilies

1 1/2 cups bread crumbs

Cook squash in 2 cups boiling water until
barely tender--5-10 minutes. Drain and cool.

Mix eggs, milk, cheese, salt, baking powder, flour,
parsley and chilies together.

Fold into squash.

Butter an oblong Pyrex 3 quart dish (about 9 x 13)

Sprinkle bottom of pan with enough breadcrumbs
to cover lightly.

Pour in squash mixture and sprinkle top with
bread crumbs (lightly)

Bake ar 350F for about 30 minutes

(Sliced tomatoes can be added to the top for a little
color and variety.

LBJ RANCH SCALLOPED POTATOES

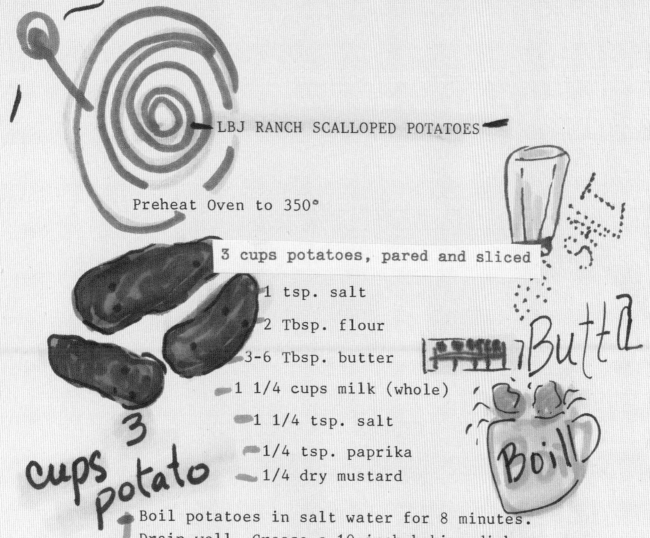

Preheat Oven to 350°

3 cups potatoes, pared and sliced

1 tsp. salt

2 Tbsp. flour

3-6 Tbsp. butter

1 1/4 cups milk (whole)

1 1/4 tsp. salt

1/4 tsp. paprika

1/4 dry mustard

Boil potatoes in salt water for 8 minutes.
Drain well. Grease a 10-inch baking dish.
Place 1/3 of potatoes in baking dish. Sprinkle

with flour and dot with butter. Add second layer
and repeat flour and butter, then final layer
and repeat.
Heat milk and add salt, paprika, and dry mustard.
Pour milk mixture over potatoes.

Bake about 35 minutes.

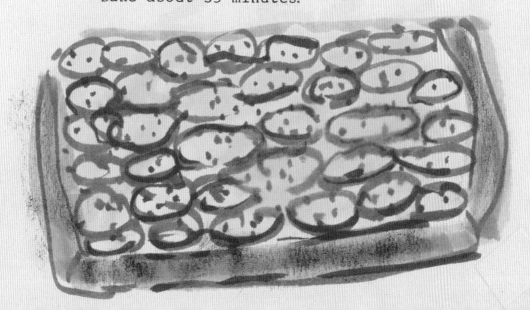

RANCH POTATO CASSEROLE

- 1 32-oz. package of frozen potato cubes or 4 cups of cubed fresh potatoes
- 1 and 1/2 sticks of butter (divided)
- 1/2 cup chopped onion
- 1 can (10 1/2 ounce) cream of chicken OR cream of mushroom soup
- 2 cups sour cream
- 2 cups grated cheddar cheese
- 2 cups corn flakes
- sprinkle of paprika

DIRECTIONS:

Thaw potatoes. Melt 1 stick butter and place in a bowl. Add potatoes and onion. Toss until mixed and pour into a 3-quart casserole dish.

In same bowl (now empty) place soup, sour cream and the cheddar cheese; stir until mixed. Pour over top of potato mixture in casserole dish, Top with flakes and the half stick of melted butter (mix them first) Sprinkle paprika on top.
Bake at 325* for one hour or until a nice golden brown.

ROSTI

President Johnson established the "Tuesday Lunch Club" specifically for setting policy on the Vietnam war. General Westmoreland and the other Chiefs of Staff had lunch every week with the President and his Secretary of Defense. He tried to make them happy by serving them a hearty meal. Rosti was a favorite!

To prepare Rosti.......
6 medium potatoes, scrubbed
1 Tbsp. butter
1 Tbsp. oil
1 tsp. salt
1/2 tsp. fresh ground white pepper

Boil potatoes in salted water for 20 minutes. Drain; refrigerate overnight.
Peel potatoes and grate coarsely.
In a saute pan, heat butter with oil. Spread potatoes evenly in the pan; season with salt and pepper.
Cook the potatoes over low heat without stirring. When brown, turn over in one piece (like a crepe) to brown the other side.
Slide onto a serving platter and serve at once.

Lady Bird's Special Lima Beans

2 pkgs. frozen baby lima beans
3 tablespoons butter
1/2 pound fresh mushrooms
4 tablespoons flour
Salt and Pepper
2 cups milk
1/2 teaspoon chili powder
1/4 cup grated sharp cheese

Cook 2 packages frozen baby lima beans in salted water.
or use fresh beans if you prefer.
Drain and set aside.
Melt 3 tablespoons butter in a saucepan and add 1/2 pound
fresh mushrooms. Cook about 5 mins. Sprinkle mushrooms
with 4 tablespoons flour. Slowly add 2 cups milk, stir and
cook until the sauce thickens and is smooth.
Remove from heat and stir in 1/4 cup grated cheese.
Add 1/2 teaspoon salt and 1/4 teaspoon pepper and the chili
powder (1/2 teaspoon).
Mix well. Drain the lima beans and gently add them but keep
them from getting mushy. Re-heat and serve hot. Serves 6.

Lady Bird's Spinach Souffle

(This recipe is a favorite of the First lady. Both the
President and Lady Bird loved spinach, in fact it was served
at the President inaugural dinner).

2 tablespoons Butter   3 eggs
2 tablespoons flour   1 cup milk
1 cup cooked spinach   1/2 cup grated Parmesan Cheese
1/4 cup choppen onion   Salt and Pepper

Make a thick white sauce of 2 Tbsp. each of butter and flour,
slowly blended with 1 cup milk. Blend in 1/2 tsp. salt and 1/2
tsp. pepper. Beat 3 egg yolks until thick and lemony and slowly
stir into the sauce. Add 1 cup well-drained chopped cooked
spinach and 1/2 cup grated cheese. Saute 1/4 cup chopped onion
and add to mixture. Beat 3 egg whites until stiff and fold into
spinach. Turn into greased casserole dish, place dish into a pan
of hot water, and bake in a preheated 350F oven 45 to 50 minutes
Serve immediately. Serves 4 to 5.

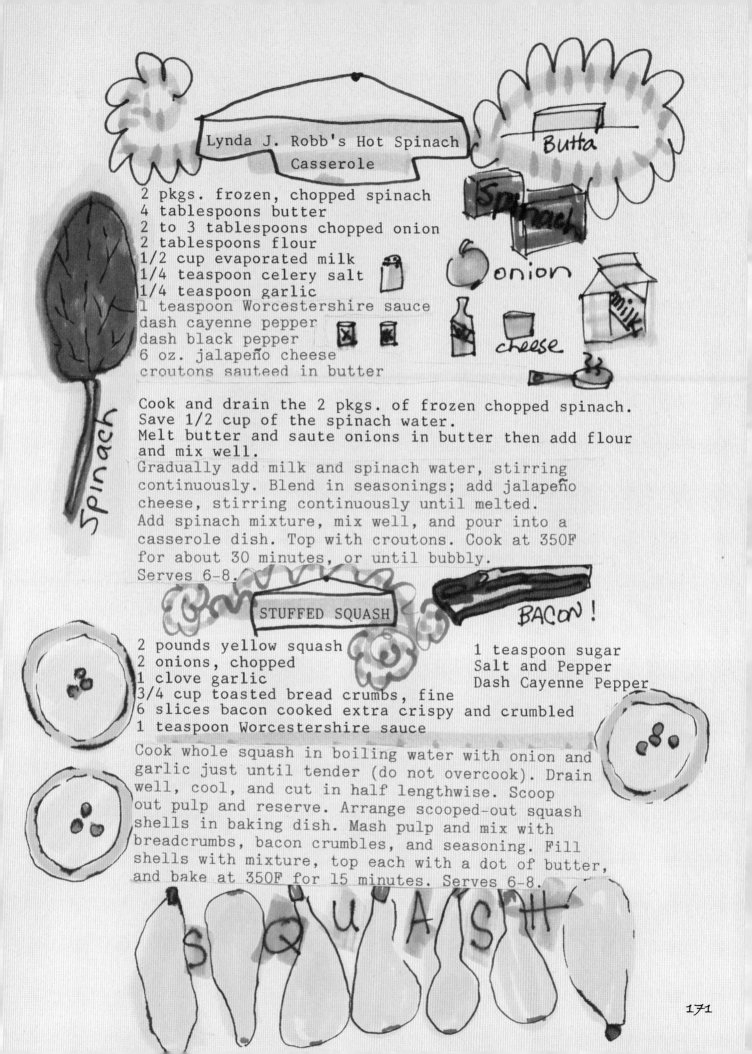

Lynda J. Robb's Hot Spinach Casserole

2 pkgs. frozen, chopped spinach
4 tablespoons butter
2 to 3 tablespoons chopped onion
2 tablespoons flour
1/2 cup evaporated milk
1/4 teaspoon celery salt
1/4 teaspoon garlic
1 teaspoon Worcestershire sauce
dash cayenne pepper
dash black pepper
6 oz. jalapeño cheese
croutons sauteed in butter

Cook and drain the 2 pkgs. of frozen chopped spinach.
Save 1/2 cup of the spinach water.
Melt butter and saute onions in butter then add flour
and mix well.
Gradually add milk and spinach water, stirring
continuously. Blend in seasonings; add jalapeño
cheese, stirring continuously until melted.
Add spinach mixture, mix well, and pour into a
casserole dish. Top with croutons. Cook at 350F
for about 30 minutes, or until bubbly.
Serves 6-8.

STUFFED SQUASH

2 pounds yellow squash
2 onions, chopped
1 clove garlic
3/4 cup toasted bread crumbs, fine
6 slices bacon cooked extra crispy and crumbled
1 teaspoon Worcestershire sauce

1 teaspoon sugar
Salt and Pepper
Dash Cayenne Pepper

Cook whole squash in boiling water with onion and
garlic just until tender (do not overcook). Drain
well, cool, and cut in half lengthwise. Scoop
out pulp and reserve. Arrange scooped-out squash
shells in baking dish. Mash pulp and mix with
breadcrumbs, bacon crumbles, and seasoning. Fill
shells with mixture, top each with a dot of butter,
and bake at 350F for 15 minutes. Serves 6-8.

"Texas usually ranks as the nation's fourth or
fifth highest producing rice-growing state, producing
about 7 percent of the nation's supply. Most Texas rice
is grown near the Colorado River. Rice farmers count on
this water to irrigate land along the Gulf Coast.

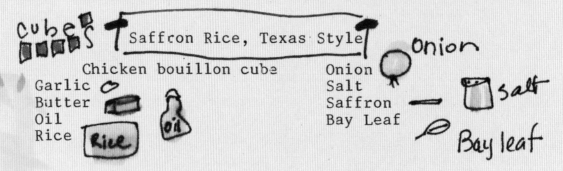

Saffron Rice, Texas Style

Chicken bouillon cube	Onion
Garlic	Salt
Butter	Saffron
Oil	Bay Leaf
Rice	

In a large skillet, saute 1 medium onion, chopped,
and 1 clove garlic, chopped, in 2 tablespoons butter
and 2 tablespoons oil, till golden brown. Add 1 1/2 cups
long grain rice and mix. Remove from heat. In a separate

pan, bring to a boil 3 3/4 cups water, 1 chicken bouillon
cube, 1 teaspoon salt, 1/8 teaspoon powdered saffron and
1 bay leaf. Add rice mixture, stirring well. Bring to
a boil again. Reduce heat, cover tightly and simmer for
20 minutes or until the liquid is absorbed. Keep covered
until ready to serve. Serves 6.

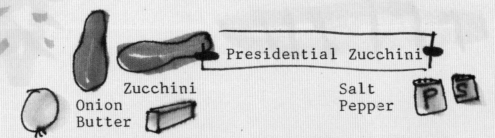

Presidential Zucchini

Zucchini	Salt
Onion	Pepper
Butter	

Cut 2 pounds zucchini into 1/4 inch slices
lengthwise and then cut slices into 1 inch pieces.
Place zucchini in a large saucepan with 1/2 cup
finely chopped onion, 2 tablespoons butter, 1 1/2
teaspoons salt and 1/2 teaspoon pepper. Stir to mix well.
Cover pan and cook over medium heat, stirring occasionally with a fork, 8 to 10 minutes or under tender.
Serves 6

State Dinners

LBJ State Dinner Facts

Johnson's first state dinner was a barbecue for 300 people catered by Walter Jetton on December 29, 1963.

When his staff realized it would be chilly that day, the sit down part was moved indoors to Stonewall High School gym that was about two miles away. Workers did an admirable job of creating an outdoorsy feeling by using bales of hay, red lanterns, red checkered table cloths, saddles, lassos, and mariachis.

According to Lady Bird's diary, there were pinto beans, delicious BBQ spareribs, coleslaw, followed by fried apricot pies with lots of hot coffee. Jetton's famous six-shooter coffee was also served. Jetton's brew was said to be so strong that a .44 pistol would float in it. The president's aides wanted to add some sophistication to the event, so they got the world's most famous pianist, Van Cliburn, another Texan, to play classical music.

Erhard presented Johnson with a bottle of 1959 Piesporter Goldtröpfchen Feinste Spätlese by Reichsgraf von Kesselstatt, a superb sweet wine. Johnson presented Erhard and his entire delegation with Stetsons.

Richard "Cactus" Pryor, a Texas humorist and KTBC employee, was master of ceremonies at this and several other barbecues. Pryor jokingly apologized to the German delegation for not finding a barbequed sauerkraut recipe.

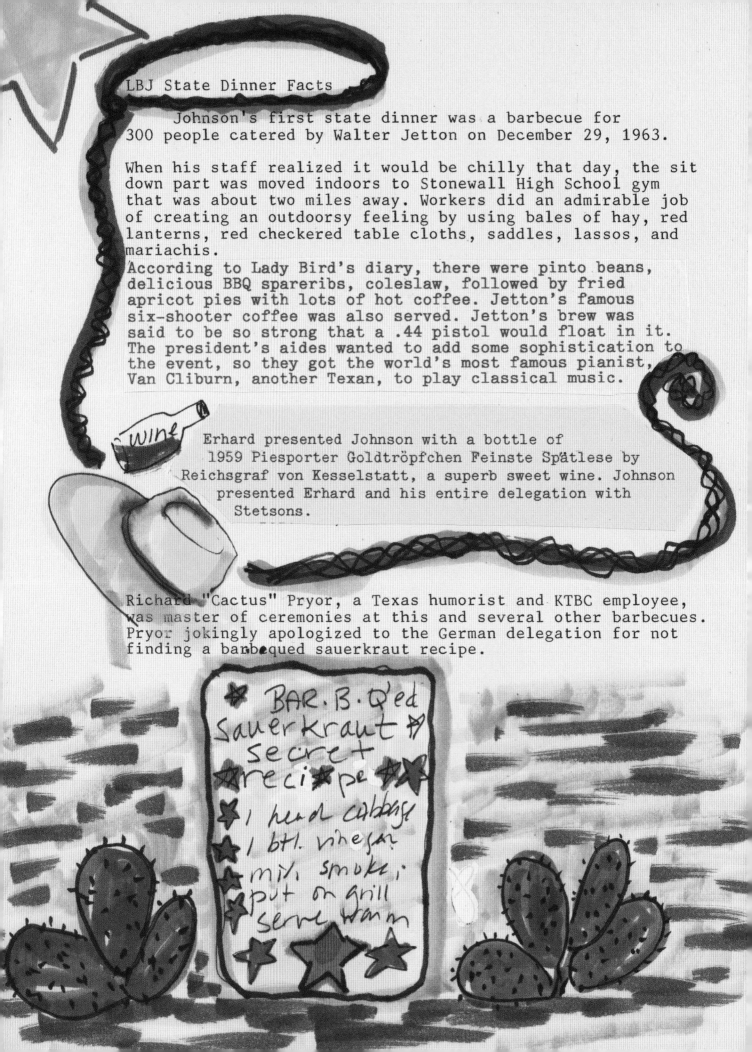

BAR·B·Q'ed
Sauerkraut
secret
recipe

1 head cabbage
1 btl. vinegar
mix, smoke,
put on grill
serve warm

White House China

Lady Bird and Lyndon Johnson decided that the
White House needed a new service to replace some of
the older ones. Mrs. Johnson worked closely with a
Tiffany & Co. designer to come up with a unique service
that reflected her commitment to "beautifying America."
On November 8, 1967, the new china was ordered: the service
would serve 140 guests at a cost of $80,028.24.
The Johnson service was the first that was not purchased
with appropriated goverment funds; an anonymous donor
through the White House Historical Association funded
the china project.

The Johnson china features hand-painted state flowers—
ten around the border of each dinner plate—representing all
50 states. There's a vintage eagle in the center of each
one. The dessert plates just have a single state flower in
the center.

Castleton China manufactured the service; the hand-painted
flowers took so long to paint that the final pieces didn't
arrive at the White House until 1972—four years into the
administration, and five years after the new service had
been announced in 1967.

Almost all of the White House service sets feature either
an eagle or a version of the presidential seal-usually at
the top- twelve o'clock position- or in the center.

The first state dinner at which the new china was used
was on May 27, 1968, honoring Prime Minister and Mrs.
John Grey Gordon of Australia. The menu included:
Chesapeake Crabmeat
Roast Duckling Bigarade
Wild Rice
Green Beans Amandine
Bibb Lettuce
Assorted Cheeses
Chocolate Mint Bettina

choc.
mint

white house
china

R.S.V.P.

According to Lady Bird's social secretary Bess Abell, "with the Johnsons, steak, of all foods, reigns supreme. It is served for breakfast, for lunch, and for state dinners (certainly not in the same day). . . . At the presidential inaugural luncheon, Texas heart of filet was served. The dinner before the big inaugural ball was private, in which bouillon, sirloin, spinach, potatoes, mixed green salad, and Baked Alaska were served. The President's food preferences seem to veer toward simple classics. Well prepared by the family cook of twenty-odd years, Mrs. Zephyr Wright."

Baked Alaska.

potato

spinach

mixed Salad

Steak

"Presidential Inaugural Dinner"

Sometimes a menu was modified to name a dish after an honored guest.

"Glacé Imelda" was a pineapple-lime sherbet dessert served President and Mrs. Marcos. The same dessert was renamed "Glacé Inonu" for the visit of Prime Minister Ismet Inonu of Turkey.

Pineapple-Lime sherbet.

The Johnsons hosted a special luncheon for former First Lady Mamie Eisenhower. Several tables were set up in the State Dining Room and each of them featured china from a different administration. The menu consisted of foods named after Presidents:

Pannequaiques
flour, egg yolk, milk, sugar, eggs, melted butter, salt. Rum/Cognac

Monroe's Quaking Jelly
LBJ's Minced Ham Turnovers
Jefferson's Filled Pannequaiques
Bouquet of Garden Vegetables
    a la John Adams
Andrew Jackson's Burnt Cream

LBJ's minced Ham Turnover

Bouquet of garden Vegetables a la John Adams

177

President and Mrs. Johnson's 30th Wedding
Anniversary

M·E·N·U

C.T.J. and L.B.J.
-- November 17, 1934

Melon of the Gods and Proscuitto

Presidential Filet of Beef
with broiled mushrooms

N.Y.A. Spinach souffle
kumquats

Mixed Green Salad a la Xochimilco

First Lady Surprise
Anniversary Cake circa 1934

Clos de la Vigne au Saint 1959

Dry Monopole 1959

Dinner for the Duke

Saturday, March 13, 1965

Crepes Tippett

Filet Mignon a la Ferdinand the Bull

Southampton Potatoes

Protocol's Favorite

Green Salad Madrid

Diplomatic Mousse

Duke Box Surprise

Wente, Pinot Chardonnay
Beaulieu, Beaumont Pinot Noir
Almaden, Blanc de Blanc, 1959

This was the menu presented at the first Senate wives' luncheon Lady Bird presided over as first lady:

Hayes Melon Cup
Veal Abigail Adams
Rice Pilaf First Lady
Asparagus Monticello
Strawberry Sherbet Dolley Madison
Demitasse

From this menu I will share with you two of the recipes served at the luncheon: the Veal Abigail Adams and the Strawberry Sherbet Dolley Madison, tested in REDBOOK'S kitchens for family-sized meals.

VEAL ABIGAIL ADAMS

1 1/2 Tbsp. melted butter

2 tsp. paprika
1 cup heavy cream
1 bay leaf
2 Tbsp. butter
2 Tbsp. flour
2 cups finely chopped cooked veal

1 1/2 cups coarsely chopped
   mushrooms
1 Tbsp. chopped chives
1 Tbsp. minced shallots
1/4 tsp. ground marjoram
few grains of cayenne pepper
3 egg whites
1/4 cup chopped blanched almonds

Heat oven to 400F. Mix the 1 1/2 tablespoons melted butter and paprika and let stand while preparing sauce. Place cream and bay leaf in saucepan and heat over low heat until bubbles appear around side of pan. Melt the 2 tablespoons butter in saucepan: blend in flour. Remove bay leaf from cream and gradually pour cream into flour mixture; cook over low heat, stirring constantly until thickened. Remove from heat; stir in paprika butter, veal, mushrooms, chives, shallots, marjoram, salt, and cayenne. Beat egg whites with beater until soft peaks form; fold into veal mixture. Spoon into individual buttered ramekins and sprinkle tops with almonds. Place ramekins in a shallow pan containing one inch of hot water. Bake 15 to 20 minutes. Serve immediately. Serves 6.

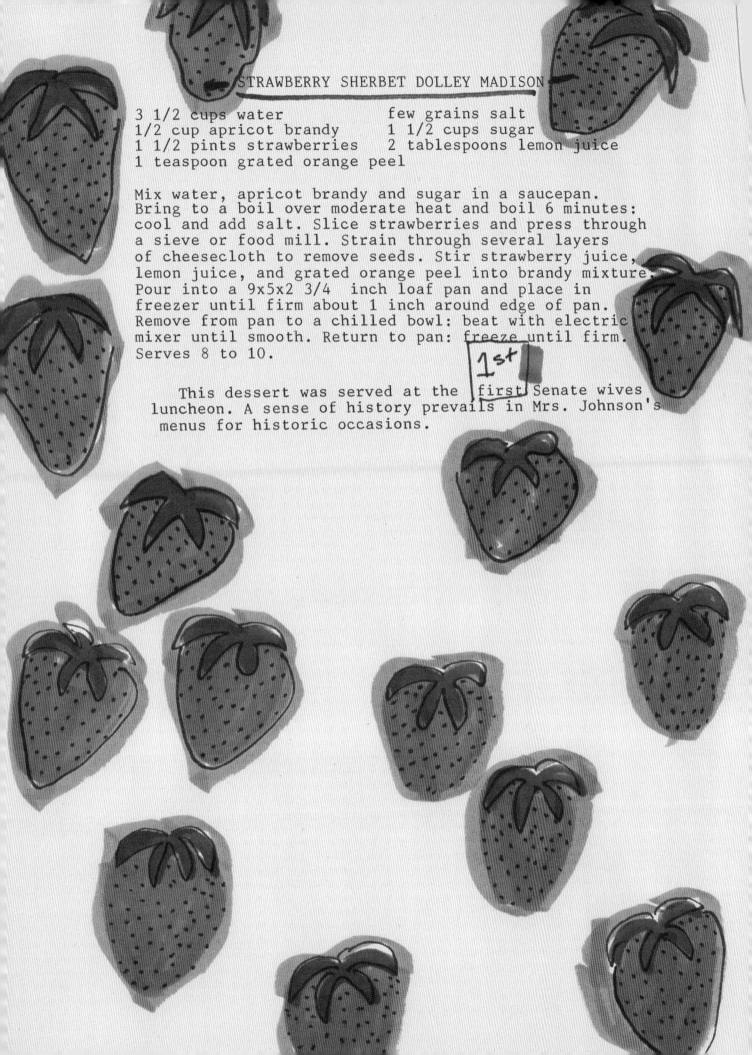

STRAWBERRY SHERBET DOLLEY MADISON

3 1/2 cups water   few grains salt
1/2 cup apricot brandy   1 1/2 cups sugar
1 1/2 pints strawberries   2 tablespoons lemon juice
1 teaspoon grated orange peel

Mix water, apricot brandy and sugar in a saucepan.
Bring to a boil over moderate heat and boil 6 minutes:
cool and add salt. Slice strawberries and press through
a sieve or food mill. Strain through several layers
of cheesecloth to remove seeds. Stir strawberry juice,
lemon juice, and grated orange peel into brandy mixture.
Pour into a 9x5x2 3/4 inch loaf pan and place in
freezer until firm about 1 inch around edge of pan.
Remove from pan to a chilled bowl: beat with electric
mixer until smooth. Return to pan: freeze until firm.
Serves 8 to 10.

This dessert was served at the first Senate wives
luncheon. A sense of history prevails in Mrs. Johnson's
menus for historic occasions.

Lobster

Lobster was served a lot . . . for example--

Lobster Thermidor...to the Prime Minister of Canada,
January 22,1964

Baby Lobster en Bellevue...to the President of Ireland,
May 27, 1964

Broiled Lobster...to guests from Iran,
June 5, 1964

Lobster Thermidor...to guests from Germany,
June 12, 1964

Cold Baby Lobster... at the Malagasy Republic dinner,
July 27, 1964

Lobster Thermidor...to the Alliance for Progress,
September 11, 1964

Broiled Lobster...at the "Woman Doer's" luncheon,
March 26, 1965

Bouchee of Lobster Newberg...at a White House dinner
March 29, 1965

Cold Baby Lobster a la White House...to guests from Korea,
May 17, 1965

Lobster Erhard...to guests from Germany,
June 4, 1965

Lobster Imperial...to guests from Germany,
December 20, 1965

Vol-au-Vent of Lobster...at a White House luncheon,
July 29, 1966

Coquille of Lobster Glace...at a small dinner
August 18, 1966

Lobster Thermidor...at lunch for former president
Dwight Eisenhower,
August 26, 1966

Cold Baby Lobster...at the Maine Beautification
Luncheon and again that evening at the Governor's Dinner,
March 18, 1967

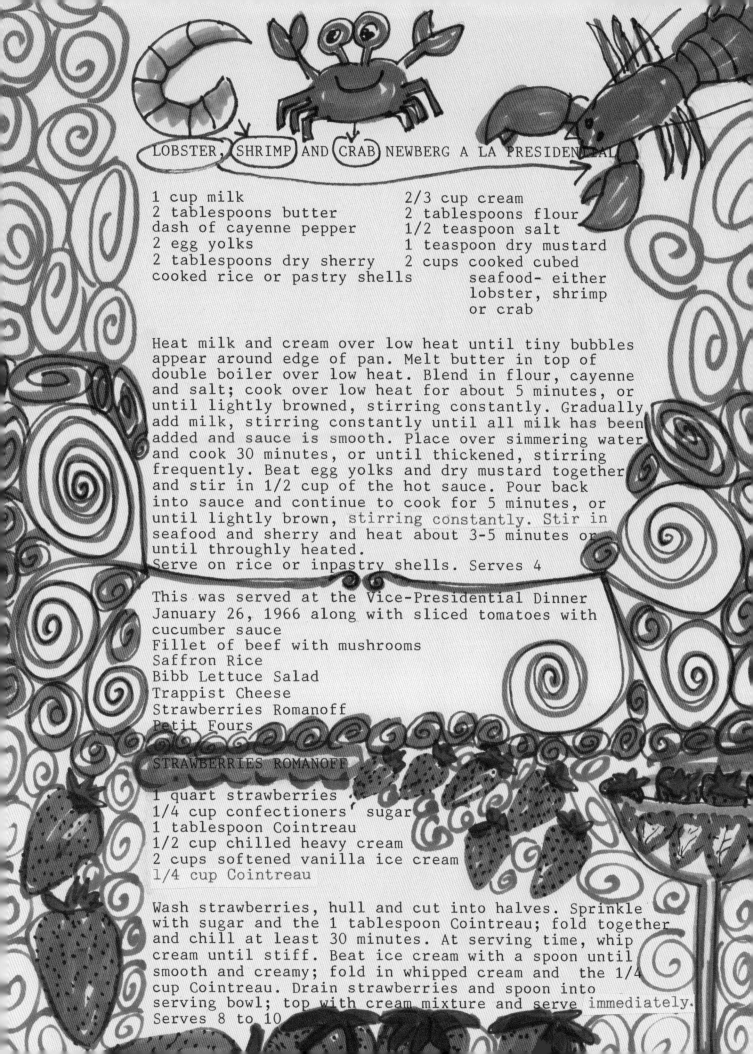

LOBSTER, SHRIMP AND CRAB NEWBERG A LA PRESIDENTIAL

1 cup milk	2/3 cup cream
2 tablespoons butter	2 tablespoons flour
dash of cayenne pepper	1/2 teaspoon salt
2 egg yolks	1 teaspoon dry mustard
2 tablespoons dry sherry	2 cups cooked cubed
cooked rice or pastry shells	seafood- either
	lobster, shrimp
	or crab

Heat milk and cream over low heat until tiny bubbles
appear around edge of pan. Melt butter in top of
double boiler over low heat. Blend in flour, cayenne
and salt; cook over low heat for about 5 minutes, or
until lightly browned, stirring constantly. Gradually
add milk, stirring constantly until all milk has been
added and sauce is smooth. Place over simmering water
and cook 30 minutes, or until thickened, stirring
frequently. Beat egg yolks and dry mustard together
and stir in 1/2 cup of the hot sauce. Pour back
into sauce and continue to cook for 5 minutes, or
until lightly brown, stirring constantly. Stir in
seafood and sherry and heat about 3-5 minutes or
until throughly heated.
Serve on rice or inpastry shells. Serves 4

This was served at the Vice-Presidential Dinner
January 26, 1966 along with sliced tomatoes with
cucumber sauce
Fillet of beef with mushrooms
Saffron Rice
Bibb Lettuce Salad
Trappist Cheese
Strawberries Romanoff
Petit Fours

STRAWBERRIES ROMANOFF

1 quart strawberries
1/4 cup confectioners' sugar
1 tablespoon Cointreau
1/2 cup chilled heavy cream
2 cups softened vanilla ice cream
1/4 cup Cointreau

Wash strawberries, hull and cut into halves. Sprinkle
with sugar and the 1 tablespoon Cointreau; fold together
and chill at least 30 minutes. At serving time, whip
cream until stiff. Beat ice cream with a spoon until
smooth and creamy; fold in whipped cream and the 1/4
cup Cointreau. Drain strawberries and spoon into
serving bowl; top with cream mixture and serve immediately.
Serves 8 to 10

An Example of: Fall and Winter Dinner Menus

with a sense of humor

Honoring the Vice President, the Chief Justice and the Speaker of the House of Representatives

Sole Nina (named for Mrs. Earl Warren, wife of the Chief Justice)

Pheasant Muriel (named for Mrs. Hubert H. Humphrey, wife of the V.P.)

Wild Rice Croquettes

Asparagus

Winter Garden Salad with Minnesota Cheese

Harriet Souffle (named for Mrs. John McCormack, wife of the Speaker)

"Big deal dinner"
AKA
State Dinners usually required guests to dress in white tie and tails. Johnson disliked this formality, so during his administration, most important functions were black tie. Johnson may have been the best dancer of all the Presidents. Jackie Kennedy called him "my favorite dance partner."

His daughter Luci also enjoyed dancing and was nicknamed "Watusi Luci."

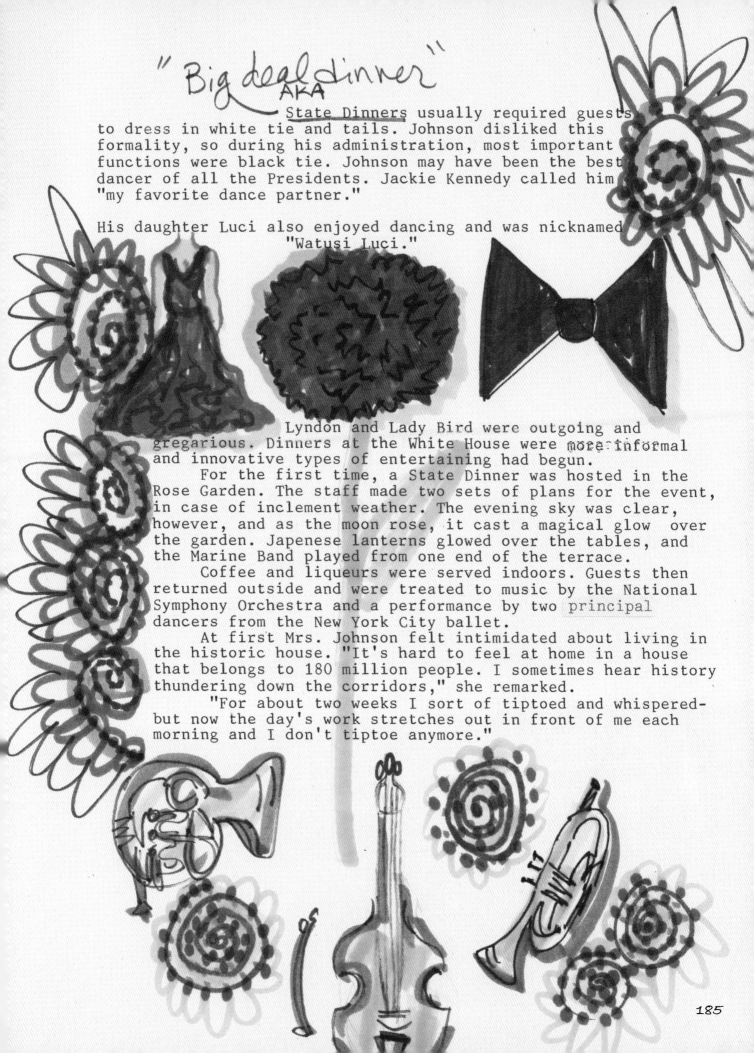

Lyndon and Lady Bird were outgoing and gregarious. Dinners at the White House were more informal and innovative types of entertaining had begun.

For the first time, a State Dinner was hosted in the Rose Garden. The staff made two sets of plans for the event, in case of inclement weather. The evening sky was clear, however, and as the moon rose, it cast a magical glow over the garden. Japenese lanterns glowed over the tables, and the Marine Band played from one end of the terrace.

Coffee and liqueurs were served indoors. Guests then returned outside and were treated to music by the National Symphony Orchestra and a performance by two principal dancers from the New York City ballet.

At first Mrs. Johnson felt intimidated about living in the historic house. "It's hard to feel at home in a house that belongs to 180 million people. I sometimes hear history thundering down the corridors," she remarked.

"For about two weeks I sort of tiptoed and whispered-but now the day's work stretches out in front of me each morning and I don't tiptoe anymore."

Salads

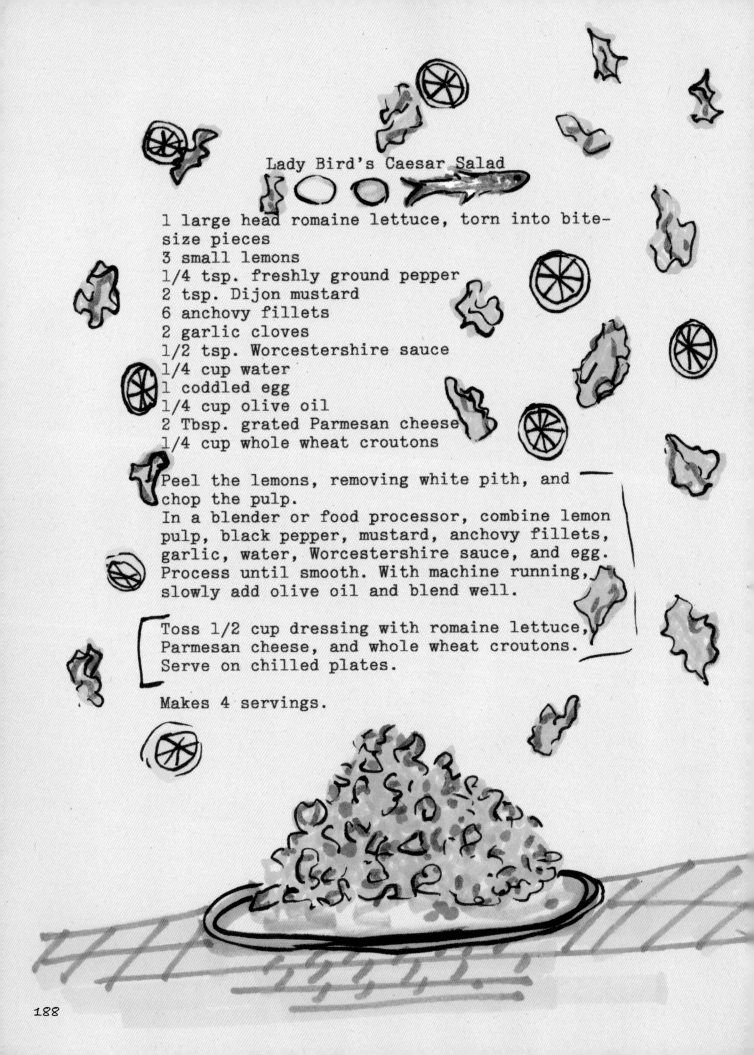

Lady Bird's Caesar Salad

1 large head romaine lettuce, torn into bite-size pieces
3 small lemons
1/4 tsp. freshly ground pepper
2 tsp. Dijon mustard
6 anchovy fillets
2 garlic cloves
1/2 tsp. Worcestershire sauce
1/4 cup water
1 coddled egg
1/4 cup olive oil
2 Tbsp. grated Parmesan cheese
1/4 cup whole wheat croutons

Peel the lemons, removing white pith, and
chop the pulp.
In a blender or food processor, combine lemon
pulp, black pepper, mustard, anchovy fillets,
garlic, water, Worcestershire sauce, and egg.
Process until smooth. With machine running,
slowly add olive oil and blend well.

Toss 1/2 cup dressing with romaine lettuce,
Parmesan cheese, and whole wheat croutons.
Serve on chilled plates.

Makes 4 servings.

Caesar Salad II

In the bottom of a wooden bowl, crush a clove
or two of garlic with salt and pepper.

Add 1 tsp. prepared mustard. Mash in two
anchovies and mix ingredients together.

Pour 2 Tbsp. olive oil into bowl, then
squeeze in the juice of a whole lemon. Mix
well.

Pile in fresh, crisp, cold romaine which has
been broken into bite-size pieces.

Break over the whole thing an egg that has
been coddled for one minute and toss, toss,
toss until every leaf has been coated.

189

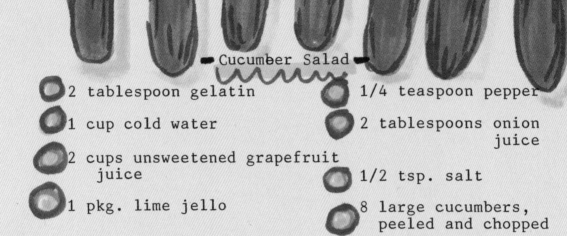

Cucumber Salad

- 2 tablespoon gelatin
- 1 cup cold water
- 2 cups unsweetened grapefruit juice
- 1 pkg. lime jello
- 1/4 teaspoon pepper
- 2 tablespoons onion juice
- 1/2 tsp. salt
- 8 large cucumbers, peeled and chopped

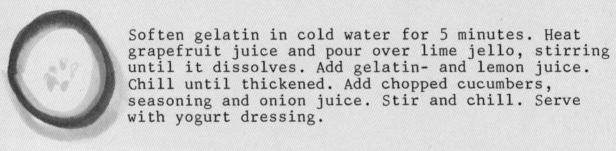

Soften gelatin in cold water for 5 minutes. Heat grapefruit juice and pour over lime jello, stirring until it dissolves. Add gelatin- and lemon juice. Chill until thickened. Add chopped cucumbers, seasoning and onion juice. Stir and chill. Serve with yogurt dressing.

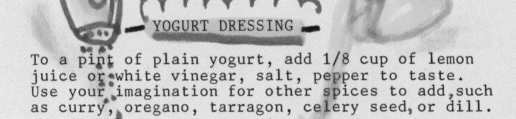

YOGURT DRESSING

To a pint of plain yogurt, add 1/8 cup of lemon juice or white vinegar, salt, pepper to taste. Use your imagination for other spices to add, such as curry, oregano, tarragon, celery seed, or dill.

TEXAS MILLIONAIRE'S MAYONNAISE

Lot of millionaires in Texas love this stuff.

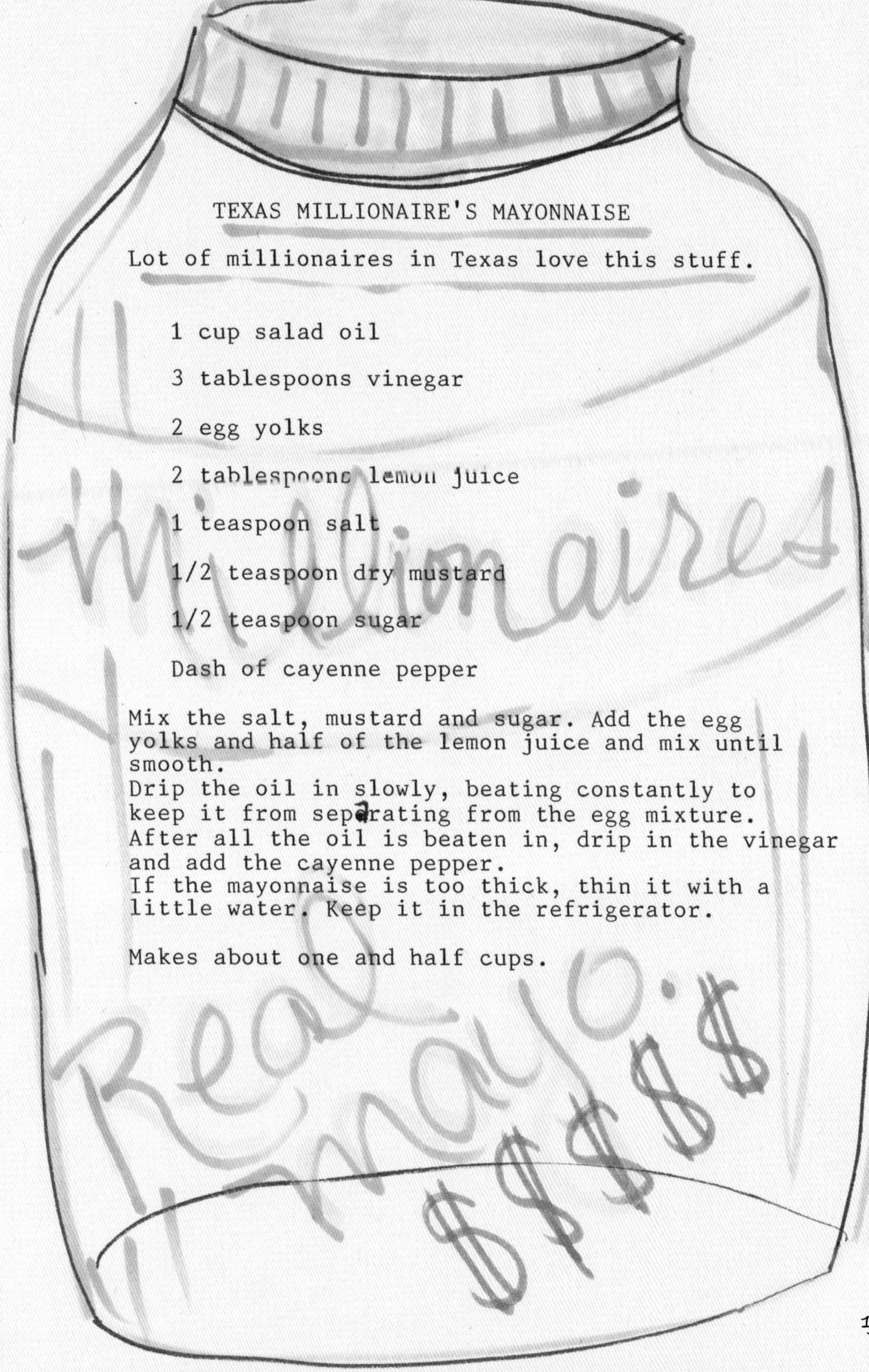

1 cup salad oil

3 tablespoons vinegar

2 egg yolks

2 tablespoons lemon juice

1 teaspoon salt

1/2 teaspoon dry mustard

1/2 teaspoon sugar

Dash of cayenne pepper

Mix the salt, mustard and sugar. Add the egg
yolks and half of the lemon juice and mix until
smooth.
Drip the oil in slowly, beating constantly to
keep it from seperating from the egg mixture.
After all the oil is beaten in, drip in the vinegar
and add the cayenne pepper.
If the mayonnaise is too thick, thin it with a
little water. Keep it in the refrigerator.

Makes about one and half cups.

191

MOLDED CRANBERRY SALAD

1 envelope unflavored gelatin
1 1/4 cups cold water
1 cup sugar
1/2 cup chopped celery
1/2 cup chopped nuts
1/2 teaspoon salt
2 cups of cranberries

Cook cranberries in 1 cup of water for 20 minutes.
Stir in sugar and cook 5 minutes longer.

Soften gelatin in 1/4 cup cold water; add to hot
cranberries and stir until dissolved. Set aside to
cool.

When mixture begins to thicken, add chopped celery,
nuts, and salt. Turn into a mold that has been rinsed
with cold water. Chill in refrigerator until firm.
Unmold on serving plate. Garnish with salad greens
if desired. Makes about 6 servings.

CRANBERRY MOLD

Macaroni Toss------------

7 ounces uncooked elbow
    macaroni
1 pkg. (10 oz.)frozen green
    peas
1 cup cubed (4 ounces) cheddar
    cheese
1 cup sliced gherkins
(small cucumber/ 3 inch)
    3/4 cup mayonnaise
1 medium onion, chopped
    salt and pepper

Cook macaroni as directed on package.
Cook peas as directed on package. Drain.
Mix macaroni, peas, cheese, gherkins, mayo
and onion; sprinkle with salt and pepper.

Cover and refrigerate at least 2 hours.
Serves 6 to 8 people.

TOSSED GARDEN SALAD WITH
LOW-FAT RANCH DRESSING

Ranch Dressing

3/4 cup low-fat cottage cheese
1/2 cup low-fat buttermilk
1/3 cup fresh lemon juice

2 cloves garlic, minced

1 large shallot, chopped
1 egg white
1/4 teaspoon freshly ground black pepper
1 tablespoon dried oregano
1 teaspoon dried thyme
1/4 cup freshly grated Parmesan Cheese

Place all ingredients in a food processor and
blend until smooth.

GARDEN SALAD

1 medium cucumber, peeled and diced
2 medium tomatoes, diced
1 head red lettuce, washed and patted dry
1 head green leaf lettuce, washed and patted dry

Tear lettuce into bite-sized pieces.
Place ingredients in large bowl and toss
with 1/2 cup dressing.

Serve chilled
Makes 4 servings

Cucumber Sauce

2/3 cup chopped peeled cucumber

1 1/2 tablespoons chopped onion

1/2 cup chilled heavy cream

1/2 cup sour cream

1/2 teaspoon salt

   Place cucumber and onion in an electric blender; blend on high speed until very finely chopped.

Chill.

Whip cream until stiff; fold in sour cream and salt.

Fold into cucumber mixture and serve immediately over sliced tomatoes or lettuce wedges.

Serves 7 or 8.

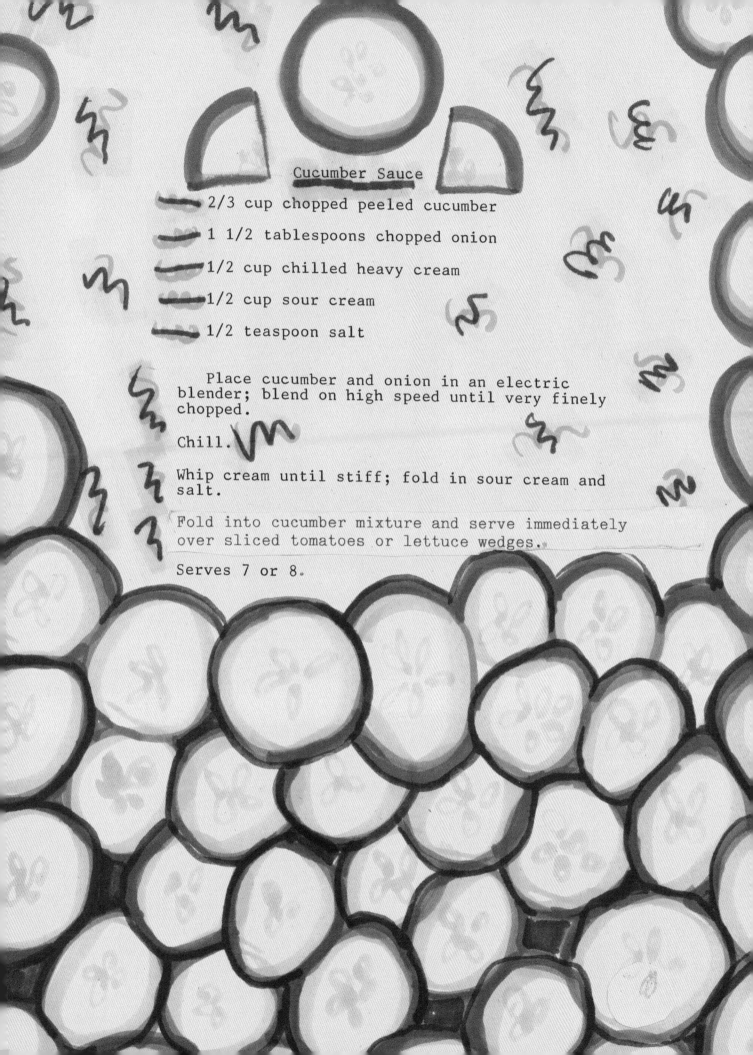

apple   spinach   bacon

Apple-Bacon Spinach Salad

1/2 lb. sliced bacon

2-3 cloves garlic, minced

1 lb. fresh spinach, washed and
    stems removed

3 large red apples, unpeeled and diced

1 bunch green onions, chopped

1 tablespoon lemon juice

2 tablespoons mayonnaise

1 cup croutons

1/2 cup grated Swiss cheese

Cook bacon until crisp, reserving 1/2 cup bacon
drippings.
Crumble bacon and set aside.

Combine drippings with garlic and set aside until
just before serving, preferably for several hours.

Tear spinach into bite-size pieces and place in
salad bowl with apples and green onions.

Combine garlic-bacon drippings mixture with lemon
juice and mayonnaise, mix well.

Pour over spinach mixture and toss.

Add crumbled bacon, croutons, and cheese, and toss
again. Serves 6-8

toss

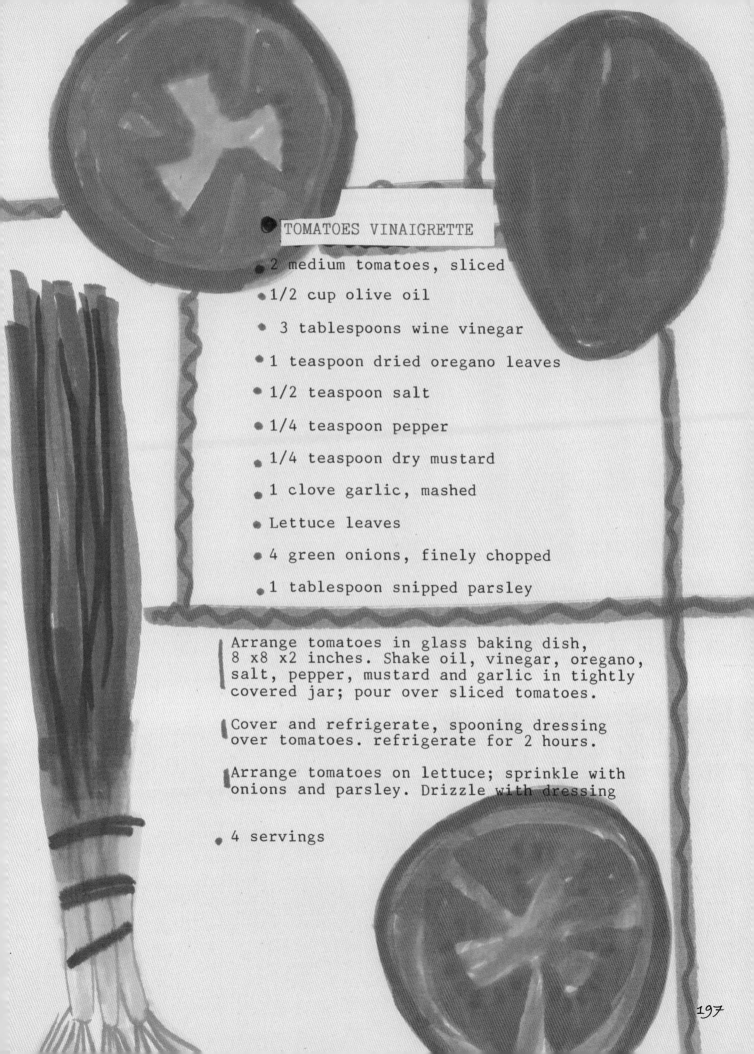

TOMATOES VINAIGRETTE

- 2 medium tomatoes, sliced
- 1/2 cup olive oil
- 3 tablespoons wine vinegar
- 1 teaspoon dried oregano leaves
- 1/2 teaspoon salt
- 1/4 teaspoon pepper
- 1/4 teaspoon dry mustard
- 1 clove garlic, mashed
- Lettuce leaves
- 4 green onions, finely chopped
- 1 tablespoon snipped parsley

Arrange tomatoes in glass baking dish,
8 x8 x2 inches. Shake oil, vinegar, oregano,
salt, pepper, mustard and garlic in tightly
covered jar; pour over sliced tomatoes.

Cover and refrigerate, spooning dressing
over tomatoes. refrigerate for 2 hours.

Arrange tomatoes on lettuce; sprinkle with
onions and parsley. Drizzle with dressing

- 4 servings

197

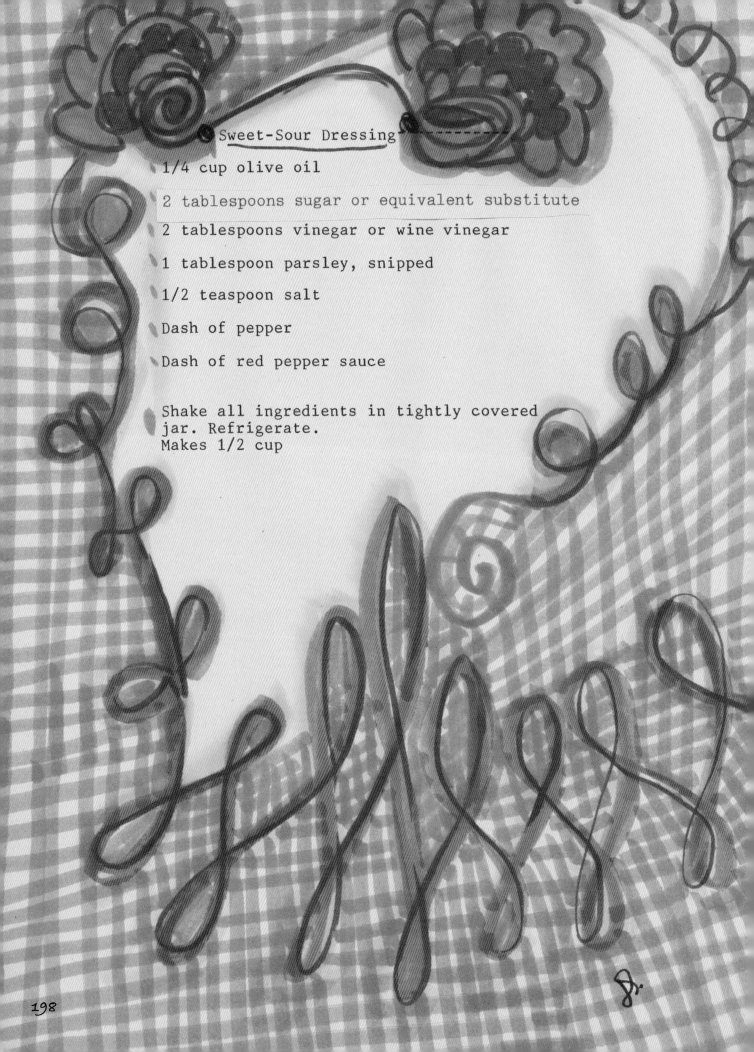

Sweet-Sour Dressing

1/4 cup olive oil

2 tablespoons sugar or equivalent substitute

2 tablespoons vinegar or wine vinegar

1 tablespoon parsley, snipped

1/2 teaspoon salt

Dash of pepper

Dash of red pepper sauce

Shake all ingredients in tightly covered
jar. Refrigerate.
Makes 1/2 cup

Mixed Vegetable Salad

Lima Beans, baby
green peas
hard cooked eggs
tomatoes
mayonnaise
carrots
beets
onions
lettuce
french dressing

Use cooked and seasoned beans, green peas,
carrots, and beets. Chill thoroughly.
Chop into bite-size pieces (or medium) all
vegetables and hard cooked eggs.

Add small amount of french dressing and enough
mayoonnaise to mix well.

Salt and Pepper to taste.

(yum!)

Peas Beet carrot Tomato Lettuce Lima Bean Peas peas Peas Peas Peas Peas

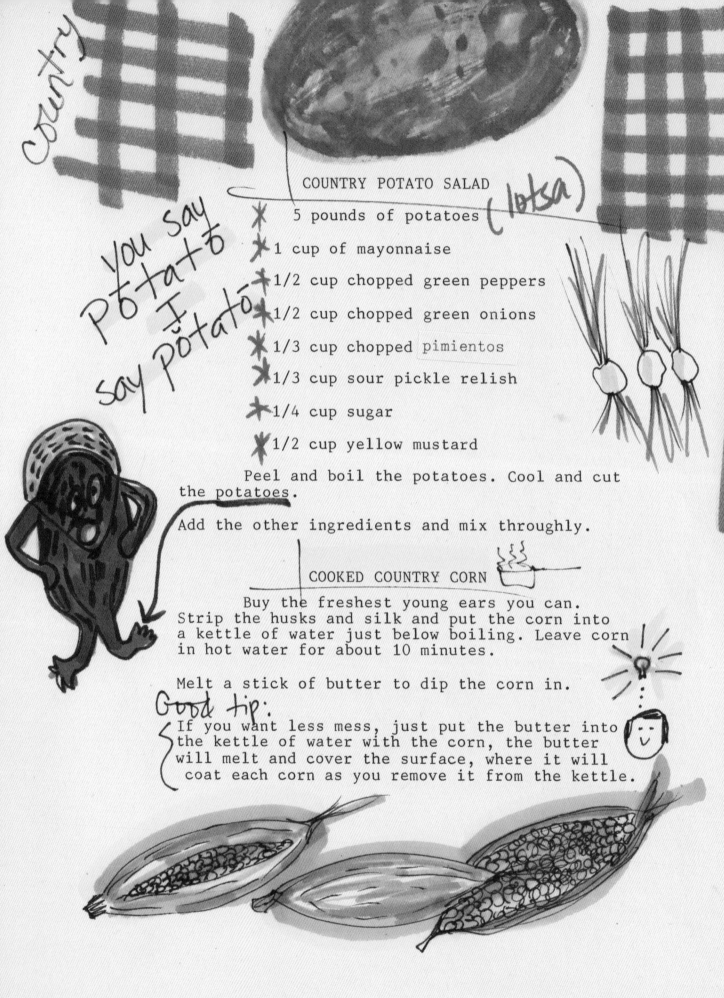

You say
Potato
I
say Potato

COUNTRY POTATO SALAD

* 5 pounds of potatoes (lotsa)

* 1 cup of mayonnaise

* 1/2 cup chopped green peppers

* 1/2 cup chopped green onions

* 1/3 cup chopped pimientos

* 1/3 cup sour pickle relish

* 1/4 cup sugar

* 1/2 cup yellow mustard

Peel and boil the potatoes. Cool and cut the potatoes.

Add the other ingredients and mix throughly.

COOKED COUNTRY CORN

Buy the freshest young ears you can. Strip the husks and silk and put the corn into a kettle of water just below boiling. Leave corn in hot water for about 10 minutes.

Melt a stick of butter to dip the corn in.

Good tip:
If you want less mess, just put the butter into the kettle of water with the corn, the butter will melt and cover the surface, where it will coat each corn as you remove it from the kettle.

Soups

Borscht

from Mrs. W.P. Hobby (Oveta Culp)..........

Chopped beets.

Chopped onion.

Chopped celery

1 cup beef broth (or water)

2 cups beef consomme

2 cups chopt cooked beets (canned or fresh)

1/2 cup chopt onion (Mrs. J. notes to use less)

1 cup chopt celery

1/4 cup lemon juice

2 teaspoons salt

1/4 teaspoon white pepper

sour cream

Combine broth and consomme, add beets, onion, and celery. Simmer 30 minutes.

Mash through a strainer. Add lemon juice, salt and pepper.

Serve hot or cold topped with a teaspoon of sour cream. Serves 8.

A LETTER

Aspen Institute for Humanistic Studies

Libby A. Cater

Special Assistant
to the President

July 1978

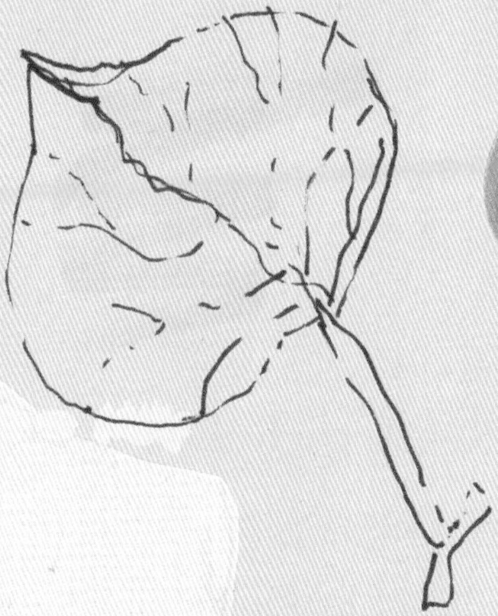

CATER WOODY CREEK SOUP:

1 can tomato soup
2 cups buttermilk
1 tsp. curry powder
1 hearty shake Worcestershire sauce
1 tsp. mustard seeds
1 peeled cucumber, chopped
2 tsp. chopped onion
Season with lemon pepper and salt.

Combine 1 can tomato soup and 2 cups buttermilk in blender with 1
tsp. curry powder, Worcestershire, and seasoning. Blend.

Add onion, cucumber, and mustard seeds. Stir.
Chill thoroughly (at least one day in advance).

ASPEN

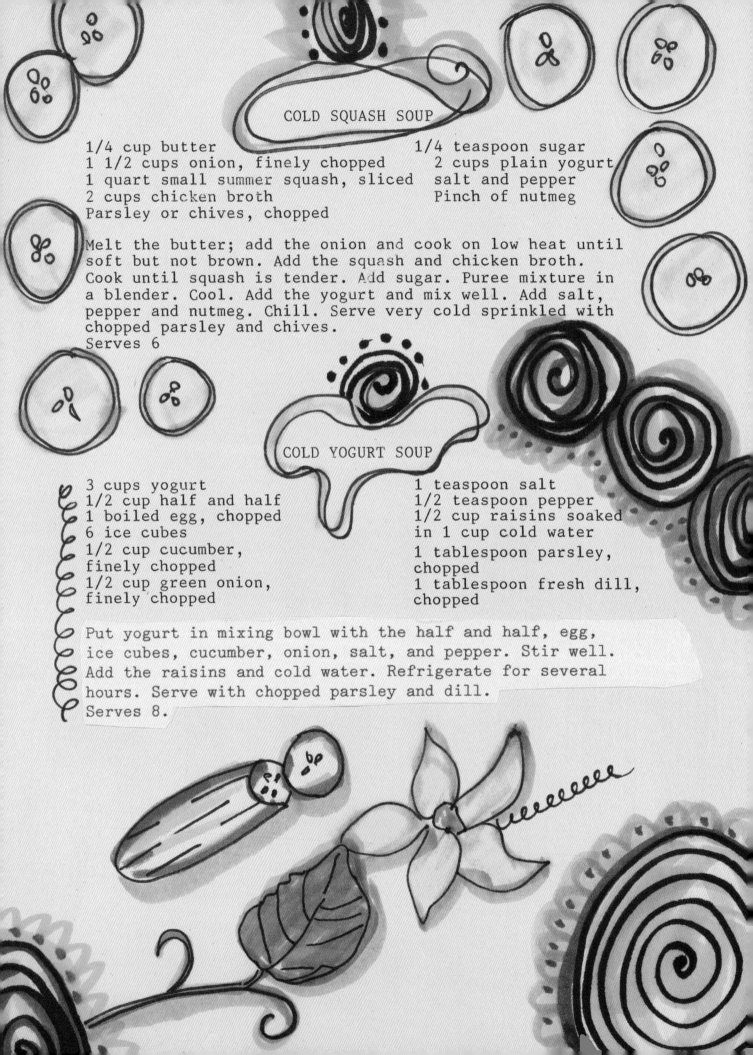

COLD SQUASH SOUP

1/4 cup butter
1 1/2 cups onion, finely chopped
1 quart small summer squash, sliced
2 cups chicken broth
Parsley or chives, chopped

1/4 teaspoon sugar
2 cups plain yogurt
salt and pepper
Pinch of nutmeg

Melt the butter; add the onion and cook on low heat until
soft but not brown. Add the squash and chicken broth.
Cook until squash is tender. Add sugar. Puree mixture in
a blender. Cool. Add the yogurt and mix well. Add salt,
pepper and nutmeg. Chill. Serve very cold sprinkled with
chopped parsley and chives.
Serves 6

COLD YOGURT SOUP

3 cups yogurt
1/2 cup half and half
1 boiled egg, chopped
6 ice cubes
1/2 cup cucumber,
finely chopped
1/2 cup green onion,
finely chopped

1 teaspoon salt
1/2 teaspoon pepper
1/2 cup raisins soaked
in 1 cup cold water
1 tablespoon parsley,
chopped
1 tablespoon fresh dill,
chopped

Put yogurt in mixing bowl with the half and half, egg,
ice cubes, cucumber, onion, salt, and pepper. Stir well.
Add the raisins and cold water. Refrigerate for several
hours. Serve with chopped parsley and dill.
Serves 8.

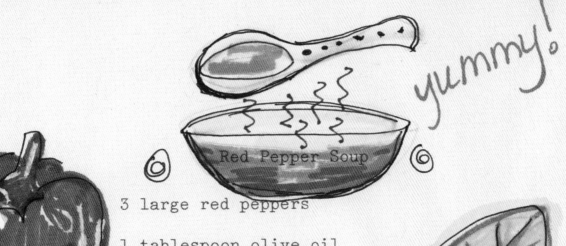

Red Pepper Soup

yummy!

3 large red peppers

1 tablespoon olive oil

1 cup chopped onion

3 cups chicken stock

1 clove garlic—minced

½ teaspoon paprika

Salt and pepper to taste

3 tablespoons tomato paste

Fresh basil or chives, chopped, for garnish

Place peppers in foil and bake at 450F
for 20 minutes, until all blackened. Remove
from foil and place in a paper bag and close it;
leave peppers in closed bag for 20 minutes.
Remove from bag and peel off skin, then chop
peppers into bite-size pieces.
Heat oil and saute onions. Add 3 cups stock,
peppers and seasonings; add tomato paste. Bring
to a boil. Cover and simmer 20 min. Garnish each
serving with chopped herbs.

Potage St. Jacques

This soup is said to have been invented for the Johnsons during the regime of Chef Haller. It may be served hot or cold. If served hot, warm up the soup before adding cream, but do not boil.

Bay Scallops
Chablis wine
Onion
Celery
Peppercorns
Salt

Thyme
Olive Oil
Flour
Heavy Cream
Parsley

In a large saucepan, combine 1 1/2 lb. diced scallops, 2 cups Chablis, 1 chopped medium onion, 1/2 cup chopped celery, 2 tsp. whole peppercorns, 1/2 tsp. salt, and 1/2 tsp. ground thyme. Bring to a boil; reduce heat, and simmer 10 minutes. In a separate saucepan, combine 2 Tbsp. olive oil and 2 Tbsp. flour; mix with a wire whisk. Strain the scallop broth and add to the oil-flour mixture. Stir well. Bring to a boil and boil for 10 minutes, stirring frequently. Take broth off the heat and add diced scallops. Allow to cool, then chill thoroughly. Before serving stir in 2 cups heavy cream.
Garnish with parsley. Serves 6.

The French Flag

Tortilla Soup
(Makes 2 qts. -- serves 8 people--1 cup)

1 Onion, chopped
1 large Jalapeño pepper, seeded and chopped
2 or 3 cloves garlic, mashed
1 Tablespoon, oil

Saute onion, pepper, and garlic in oil until limp

Then ADD: 1 one-pound can stewed tomatoes

4-6 cups stock (bouillon cubes or diluted canned
stock)

1 can tomato soup

STIR THOROUGHLY

ADD:

1 tsp. each ground cumin, chili powder, salt,
and sugar.

1/2 tsp. lemon pepper

1 to 2 tsp. each of Worcestershire and Tabasco
(adjust to taste)

Simmer above ingredients for one to one and half
hours, uncovered, between medium and low heat.

The last ten minutes of cooking add:

4 tortillas cut in thin strips- like noodles.

Serve soup as follows:

Grated sharp cheese in the bottom of the bowl,
ladle hot soup over the cheese - then top with some
chopped avocado and a dollop of sour cream.

-----Anne Clark

Jalapeño
pepper

207

Tortilla Soup Giraud

Ingredients:

1 1/2 onions, chopped
1 bell pepper, diced
2 potatoes, diced
2 carrots, diced
1/4 celery bunch, diced
3 1/2 quarts chicken stock
3/4 cup garbanzo beans
1 lb. chicken breasts, cooked and chopped
2 Tbsp. chili powder
1 Tbsp. comino (cumin)
1 tsp. white pepper
1 tsp. garlic powder
2 Tbsp. cilantro, chopped

Method:

---- Saute onion and bell pepper for 1 minute
---- Add carrots, celery, potatoes and saute for 2 min.
---- Add HOT chicken stock and simmer for 5 to 10 mins.
---- Add seasonings
---- Add chopped chicken and cilantro
---- Garnish with fried tortilla strips, lime & Avocado

Makes about 1 gallon

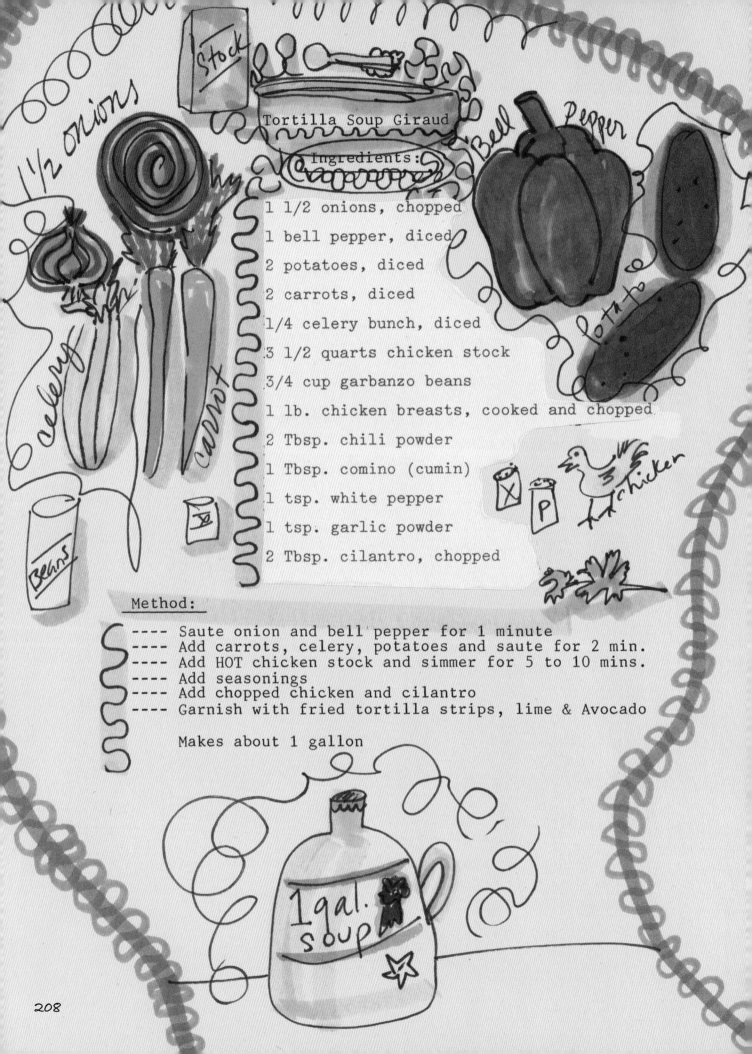

Papaya cross section showing orange flesh and black seeds.

Outside shell of Papaya

Leaf

mango

Tropical Fruit Soup

2 medium papayas, chilled

1 large mango, chilled

1 cup unsweetened apple juice, cold

1 cup nonfat-skim milk, cold

1 tablespoon honey

pinch ground cinnamon

thin julienned strips lemon zest to garnish

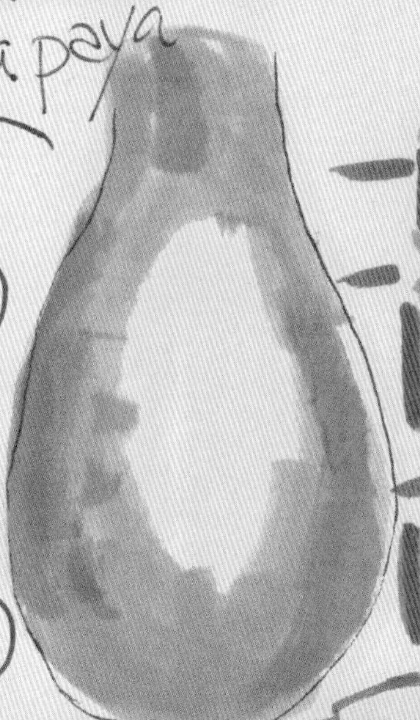

Cut papayas in half lengthwise and scoop out seeds.

Carefully remove flesh, leaving 1/4 inch pulp still attached to the skin. Reserve pulp and papaya shell. Peel and pit mango and cut into large pieces. Add to papaya pulp (you should have a total of about 2 cups of pulp).

Puree pulp, apple juice, milk, honey and cinnamon in a blender. Pour into papaya shells, garnish with lemon zest and serve at once.

Serves 4.

Honey

U.S. SENATE BEAN SOUP

Governor   Connally, who was critically
wounded by a bullet from the gun of the assassin
who killed President Kennedy, liked this soup so much
when he was in the U.S. Senate that it became famous
in Washington. He recommended the soup to LBJ's chef.

2 cups white beans, soaked overnight
Ham bone with meat on it
3 quarts water
1/2 cup cooked mashed potatoes
3 onions, chopped fine
1 bunch celery, stalks and tops, chopped fine
1 clove garlic, minced
1/4 cup finely chopped parsley

Simmer beans, ham bone, and water for two hours.
Add mashed potatoes when beans are half cooked. Stir
until mixed. Add remaining ingredients. Simmer another
hour. Remove bone. Chop ham from it and add to soup
before serving.

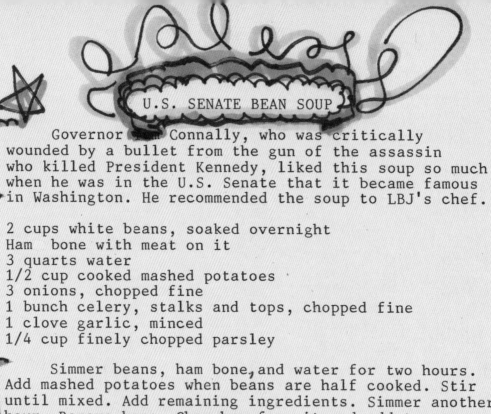

Paris (TEXAS) Onion Soup

2 quarts sliced onions	3/4 pound butter
1 teaspoon salt	1/2 teaspoon pepper
1 quart milk	1 pint cream
2 cups heavy chicken broth	

Simmer onions in butter 45 minutes. Season to
taste. Add milk, cream, and chicken broth. Pour over
toast in bottom of oven-proof soup bowls. Sprinkle
with grated Parmesan cheese or wedges of goat's
milk cheese. Put under broiler until cheese melts
and bubbles.

onions are good for you.
a 2019 study in the Asia Pacific
Journal of Clinical Oncology found
that the risk of colorectal
cancer was 79% lower in those
that ate allium vegetables, such as
onions (regularly)

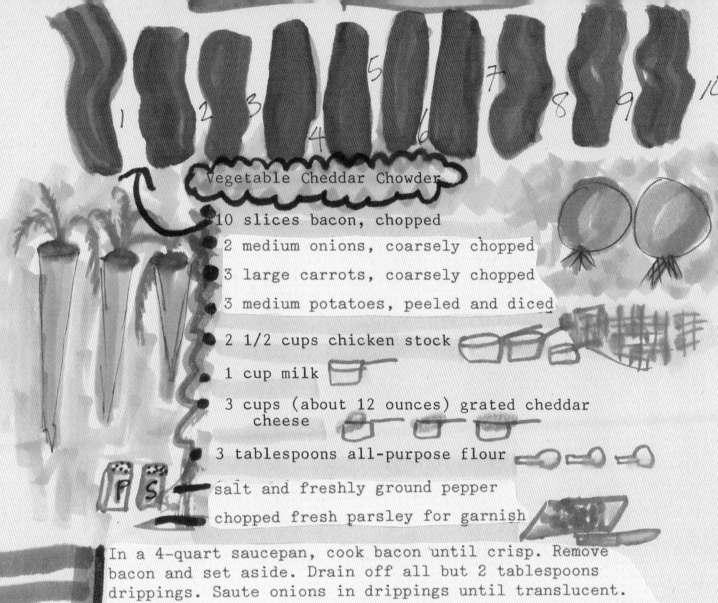

Vegetable Cheddar Chowder

- 10 slices bacon, chopped
- 2 medium onions, coarsely chopped
- 3 large carrots, coarsely chopped
- 3 medium potatoes, peeled and diced
- 2 1/2 cups chicken stock
- 1 cup milk
- 3 cups (about 12 ounces) grated cheddar cheese
- 3 tablespoons all-purpose flour
- salt and freshly ground pepper
- chopped fresh parsley for garnish

In a 4-quart saucepan, cook bacon until crisp. Remove bacon and set aside. Drain off all but 2 tablespoons drippings. Saute onions in drippings until translucent. Add bacon, carrots, potatoes, and stock. Bring to a boil; reduce heat, cover, and simmer 15 minutes, or until potatoes are tender. Stir in milk. Toss together cheese and flour until cheese is coated. Add to soup and heat, stirring, until cheese melts. Season with salt and pepper. Garnish each serving with chopped parsley.

Simon Pearce Velveeta Cheddar Soup

- ✓ 3 quarts chicken stock
- ✓ 1 small onion, chopped
- ✓ 2 cloves garlic, minced
- ✓ 5 oz. butter
- ✓ 6 oz. flour
- ✓ 2 cups half-and-half
- ✓ 1 cup heavy cream
- ✓ 1 teaspoon finely chopped thyme
- ✓ 2 bay leaves
- ✓ salt and fresh-ground pepper
- ✓ 1 lb. grated Velveeta cheese
- ✓ 1 cup grated carrot
- ✓ 1 cup minced celery

Thumbs UP for da carrot!

SOUP BAY LEAF

onion

Butter

flour

BOIL

Bring stock to a boil.

Melt butter in heavy stock pot. Add onions and garlic; cook until translucent. Add flour to butter/onion mixture; stir to combine well. Turn heat very low and cook mixture about 15 minutes, stirring occasionally.

Add hot stock ⅓ at a time-stir with whisk until smooth. Season with thyme, bay leaves, salt, and pepper. Cook over low heat till smooth and creamy. Add grated cheese.

Cook carrots and celery until tender; add to mixture. Add half-and-half and cream; heat to serving temperature.

SERVE HOT. DO NOT OVERHEAT.

CHEESE velveeta

Desserts

A presidential favorite...rum pie. A story

Q. The president, having finished his pie, noted that
General Wheeler had eaten only a few bites of his.
"Buzz,'the president whispered, getting the chairman's
attention......
"Yes, Mr. President, " General Wheeler responded.
"Are you through with your pie?"
"Yes, Mr President."
"May I have it?"
"Yes, Mr. President."
"Whereupon the President, under the eaglelike gaze of
Mrs. Johnson, ate what remained of General Wheeler's pie.

From Lyndon: An Oral Biography,
by Merle Miller (542)

RUM PIE

Ingredients

2 prepared pie crusts
6 egg yolks
1 cup white sugar
1 (.25 ounce) package unflavored gelatin
1/2 cup cold water
2 cups heavy cream
1/2 cup rum

Directions

Pour the cold water into a small bowl and sprinkle
with the gelatin. Set aside and allow the gelatin
to soften.

Combine the egg yolks and sugar in a heat-proof
mixing bowl. Beat with a hand mixer or a whisk until
the mixture is thick and lemon-colored. Set the bowl
over a pot of water (simmering) on the stove and
cook, stirring constantly, about 5 minutes. The
mixture should feel hot to the touch and have reached
145 degrees F on a thermometer.

Remove the bowl from the heat and mix in the gelatin.
Stir until the gelatin dissolves and let mixture cool
to room temperature.
Whip the heavy cream to form peaks, stir in rum.
Fold whipped cream into the egg mixture. Pour into
pie crusts. Chill pie overnight.

T·a·p·i·o·c·a P·u·d·d·i·n·g

President Johnson was very fond of tapioca pudding and was always available for dessert. He preferred the pudding cold, without any topping. Occasionally the pudding was prepared using half sugar and half sugar substitute in order to reduce calories.

Tapioca Pudding

- 3 cups milk
- 5 tablespoons instant tapioca
- 2 teaspoons vanilla extract
- 6 tablespoons sugar
- 1/4 teaspoon salt
- 2 egg yolks
- 3 egg whites, at room temp.

Bring 2 1/2 cups of the milk to a boil. Using a wire whisk stir tapioca into boiling milk. Reduce heat, and cook over very low heat, stirring constantly, until thick (about 3 to 4 minutes). Remove from heat and add vanilla, sugar and salt. Mix egg yolks with the remaining 1/2 cup of milk, and stir into tapioca mixture. In a clean bowl beat the egg whites until stiff: fold into the tapioca mixture. Pour into a serving dish and refrigerate. Serve chilled, plain or topped with RASPBERRY SAUCE and whipped cream.

Raspberry Sauce

- 1 10-ounce package frozen raspberries, defrosted

Puree raspberries in blender: strain.
Pour over puddings, ice cream, or frozen fruit souffles.

Makes 1 1/2 cup

Raspberries
✓ Low in saturated FAT
✓ High-Fiber
✓ Sodium Free
✓ Gluten-Free

yum!

Lady Bird's German
Chocolate Cake and
Coconut-Pecan Filling and Frosting
(adapted from a Baker's Chocolate recipe)

1 pkg. Baker's Chocolate (4 1-oz. squares)
1/2 cup boiling water
1 cup softened butter
2 cups sugar
4 unbeaten egg yolks
1 tsp. vanilla
2 1/2 cups sifted cake flour
1 tsp. baking soda
1/2 tsp. salt
1 cup buttermilk
4 egg whites, beaten until stiff

Melt chocolate in 1/2 cup boiling water. Cool.

Cream butter and sugar until light and fluffy.
Add egg yolks one at a time, beating after each.
Add vanilla and melted chocolate and mix until blended.
Sift flour with baking soda and salt. Add sifted dry
ingredients to chocolate mixture alternately with
buttermilk, beating after each addition until batter
is smooth.

Fold in stiffly beaten egg whites. Pour batter into
three 9-inch round layer pans that have been greased
and floured

Bake in 350F oven for 35-40 minutes.

Coconut-Pecan Filling and Frosting

1 cup evaporated milk
1 cup sugar
3 egg yolks, slightly beaten
1 stick butter (softened)
1 teaspoon vanilla
1 1/3 cups flaked coconut
1 cup chopped pecans

Combine evaporated milk, sugar, egg yolks, butter
and vanilla in a saucepan. Cook over medium heat 12 min.
stirring constantly, until mixture thickens. Remove from
heat. Add coconut and pecans. Stir until well mixed.

CAKE, MOIST, CHOCOLATY, CAKE

BEST EVER

FRIED APPLE PIE

President Johnson loved these !

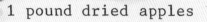

1 pound dried apples

1 pound butter

1 pound sugar

1/2 cup thinly sliced orange

1/4 lemon, sliced thin

Tough pastry, rolled out

Cover apples, orange and lemon with water and
cook over the fire for about 15 minutes- until
they are tender. Remove from the heat and add the
butter and sugar, mixing well. Let the apple mixture
chill.
Roll out the pastry and cut it in 4-inch circles.
Add 2 tablespoons of the apple mixture to each circle
and fold over. press the edges together with fork prongs.

Fry in deep fat until brown.

"Fried pies are as old as the hills and have

never been altered in any way. Some people use pie

dough. Others use a biscuity dough. Oh! What I wouldn't
do with a couple right now!"

someone
"special"

---A Dallas Socialite

Best EVER choc. CAKE!

Luci's Chocolate Layer Cake

- 3 ounces/squares of unsweetened chocolate
- 1 stick butter
- 1 cup sugar
- 3 egg yolks
- 2 cups flour
- 2 teaspoons baking powder
- 1/4 teaspoon salt
- 1 teaspoon vanilla extract
- 1 cup milk (room temp.)
- 3 egg whites (room temp.)
- Pinch of cream of tartar

Preheat oven to 350F. Grease 2 9-inch pans and dust lightly with flour.

Melt chocolate in a double boiler over hot water; remove from heat and set aside to cool.

In a large mixing bowl cream butter with sugar and beat in egg yolks one at a time.

Mix in cooled melted chocolate.

In a separate bowl sift together flour, baking powder, and salt.

In a small mixing bowl mix together vanilla and milk. Add to chocolate mixture alternately with dry Ingredients, stirring after each addition until batter is smooth.

In a clean bowl beat egg whites with cream of tartar until stiff. Gently fold into batter.

Pour batter into the greased and floured pans. Bake in hot (400F) oven for about 25 minutes. Cake is done when it shrinks slightly from edges of the pan. Let cool 5 minutes before removing from pans.

Royal Icing for the Cake

4 egg whites   2 tsp. light corn syrup
juice of 2 lemons   7 cups confectioners' sugar

Beat egg whites with lemon juice until stiff. Add corn syrup and continue beating. (continued next page)

Royal Icing (con't)

Gradually add confectioners' sugar, beating
constantly until smooth.
Use icing at once, or cover with a damp cloth and
keep cool to prevent premature hardening.

PRESIDENT JOHNSON'S CHEWY MACAROONS

2 egg whites, at room temperature
A pinch of salt
1/2 cup of sugar
1 cup sweetened shredded coconut
1/2 teaspoon vanilla extract

Preheat oven to 325. Lightly grease several baking sheets
Beat egg whites with salt until stiff
Gradually beat in sugar until stiff, shiny peaks form
Drop by teaspoonfuls onto prepared sheets: leave ample
space (2 inches) between spoonfuls to allow space for
cookie to spread evenly while baking
Bake on middle shelf for 20 minutes, or until golden
brown
Cool on wire rack before serving. Store in airtight
container in refrigerator.

--President Johnson loved these cookies on the chewy
side and soft.

SO ALL AMERICAN....

LBJ's Apple Pie

- 6 Winesap Apples
- 1 cup sugar
- 2 Tbs. flour
- juice of one lemon
- 1 stick of butter
- Pastry for 2 crust pie

Peel and slice apples into unbaked pastry shell.
Mix sugar and flour and sprinkle over apples.

Sprinkle lemon juice over apples and dot with 3/4
of the butter. Top with crust, sealing edges;
sprinkle crust with sugar and dot with remaining
butter.

Bake in 350F oven about 1 hour, or until brown.

Cream Pie

- 1 cup sugar
- 1/2 cup flour or
  3 1/2 Tbsp. cornstarch
- 1/2 tsp. salt
- 3 eggs, separated
- 2 Tbsp. Butter
- 1 tsp. vanilla

Mix together 2/3 cup of sugar, flour and salt; gradually
stir in milk and cook over boiling water for 10 mins, (double boiler)
stirring constantly until mixture thickens. Stir small
amount into slightly beaten egg yolks; then gradually
pour into thickened milk and cook about 2 minutes, stirring
constantly. Add butter and vanilla and cool slightly.
Turn into baked pastry shell. Cover with meringue made by
gradually beating remaining 1/3 cup of sugar into stiffly
beaten egg whites. Brown delicately.

For Lemon Pie

Use 1 1/2 cups milk and 1/2 cup fresh lemon juice.
Add lemon juice to egg and sugar.

220

 SAND BARS

1 1/2 cups butter

6 tbsp. sugar

1/2 teaspoon vanilla

4 1/2 cups flour

1 teaspoon salt

2 1/4 cups coarsely chopped pecans

6 cups powdered sugar, to roll cookies in

Cream the butter until light and fluffy. Add granulated sugar and cream well.

Add vanilla and mix. Sift flour and salt together. Gently mix in chopped nuts until evenly distributed.

Shape into bars about 3 inches long and 1/2 inch thick. Shape to a point on the end.

NOTE: This is a crumbly mixture and if it will not stick together add a little melted butter.

Place on lightly greased baking sheet and bake for 20 minutes at 350F.

Put the 2 pounds of powdered sugar into a bowl, and as soon as the sand bars come from the oven roll in powdered sugar until entirely covered. Re-roll again in sugar.

Yield: 5 dozen medium sand bars

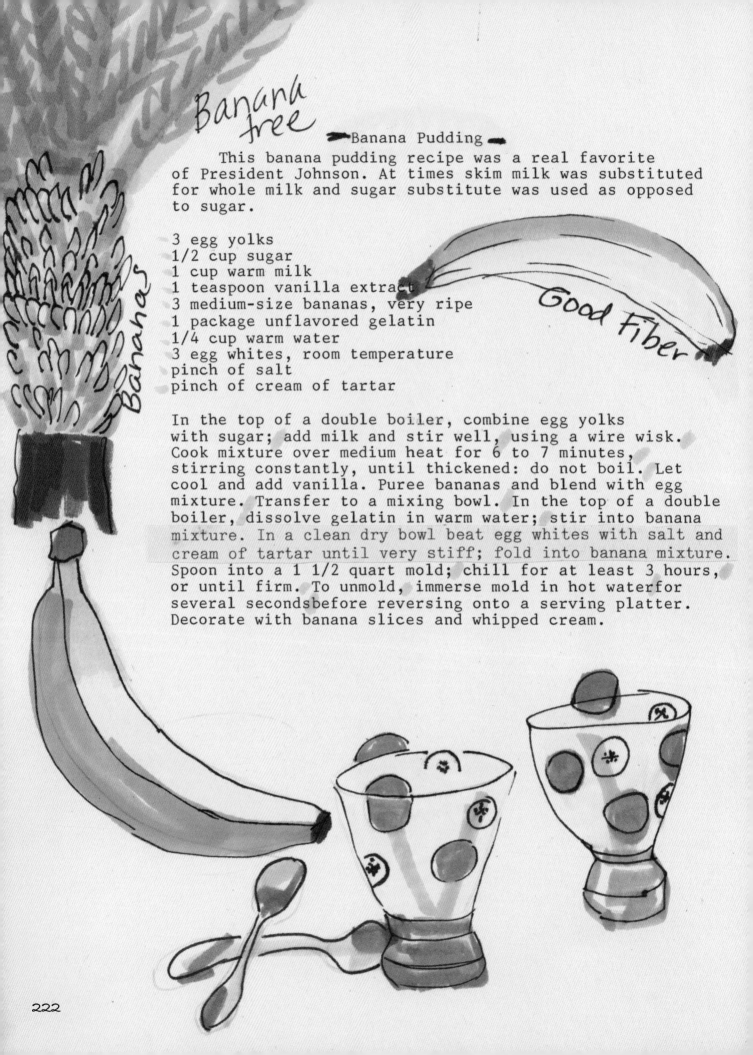

Banana tree

— Banana Pudding —

This banana pudding recipe was a real favorite of President Johnson. At times skim milk was substituted for whole milk and sugar substitute was used as opposed to sugar.

Good Fiber

Bananas

3 egg yolks
1/2 cup sugar
1 cup warm milk
1 teaspoon vanilla extract
3 medium-size bananas, very ripe
1 package unflavored gelatin
1/4 cup warm water
3 egg whites, room temperature
pinch of salt
pinch of cream of tartar

In the top of a double boiler, combine egg yolks with sugar; add milk and stir well, using a wire wisk. Cook mixture over medium heat for 6 to 7 minutes, stirring constantly, until thickened: do not boil. Let cool and add vanilla. Puree bananas and blend with egg mixture. Transfer to a mixing bowl. In the top of a double boiler, dissolve gelatin in warm water; stir into banana mixture. In a clean dry bowl beat egg whites with salt and cream of tartar until very stiff; fold into banana mixture. Spoon into a 1 1/2 quart mold; chill for at least 3 hours, or until firm. To unmold, immerse mold in hot waterfor several secondsbefore reversing onto a serving platter. Decorate with banana slices and whipped cream.

LEMON SQUARES

--another favorite of Lady Bird Johnson's and she served them often!!!

Crust:
2 cups flour
1/2 cup sugar   1 cup butter

Custard

2 cups sugar   3 eggs beaten
1 teaspoon baking powder   Juice and rind of 2
4 tablespoons flour   lemons

Mix the three crust ingredients.
Pat into a 9 X 18-inch jelly roll pan.
Bake at 350 degrees, about 15 minutes or until crust is light brown.

Mix custard ingredients in order given; pour over baked crust.

Bake for 15 to 20 minutes or until set.
Sprinkle with powdered sugar.

Makes 5 to 6 dozen

This is from Lady Bird's designer friend, Ms. Mollie Parnis Livingston.

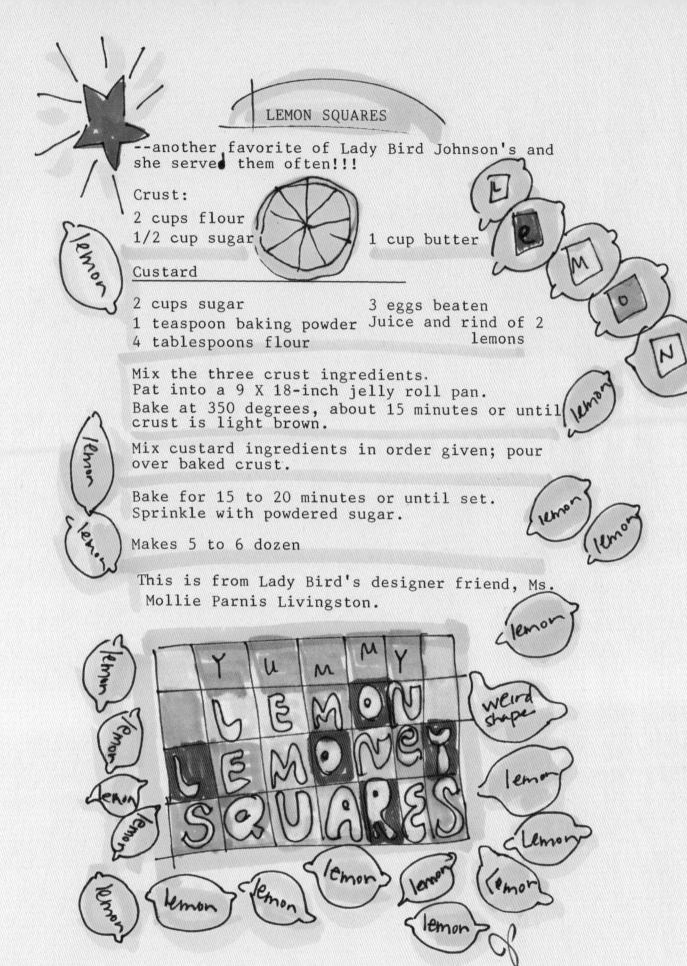

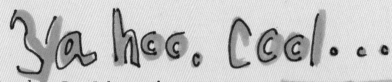

Mrs. Lyndon B. Johnson's Recipe for Texas Cookies

• Blend together 1/2 cup of butter and 1 cup of
  granulated sugar.
• Add one egg and 1 Tbs. of fresh cream.
• Grate rind of lemon and 1/2 tsp. of lemon flavoring
  and add to mixture.
• Add 1 1/2 cups of flour, 1/2 teaspoon of salt
  and 1 teaspoon of baking powder. Mix well.
• Chill for 2 to 3 hours- or over night in fridge.

• Roll out very thin and cut with a cookie cutter
  shaped like TEXAS!!. Bake 8 to 10 mins. in 375F
  oven.

T.E.X.A.S

#1
1 cup
sugar
1/2
cup
butter

#2
1 egg
1 tbsp.
cream

#3
→ lemon
flavoring
grate rind
of lemon
Add

Add

Add

in Blend
bowl

TEXAS
COOKIE
cutter.

mix it
all up

#4
1 1/2
cup flour
1/2 teaspoon salt
1 teaspoon
baking powder

orange
icing.

Add

Mrs. Lyndon B. Johnson's Recipe for

Brandied Fruit

Dried Apricots

Golden Raisins

Pineapple Chunks

Canned Peaches

Whole Cranberries

Drain pineapple chunks, peaches, and cranberries well.

Layer fruit, ending with cranberries.

Dust with brown sugar.

Dab with sweet butter.

Pour dry sherry over all fruit.

Bake in 350F oven for 20 min.

Pour a glass of sherry to drink while you are at it! Cheers!

SHERRY

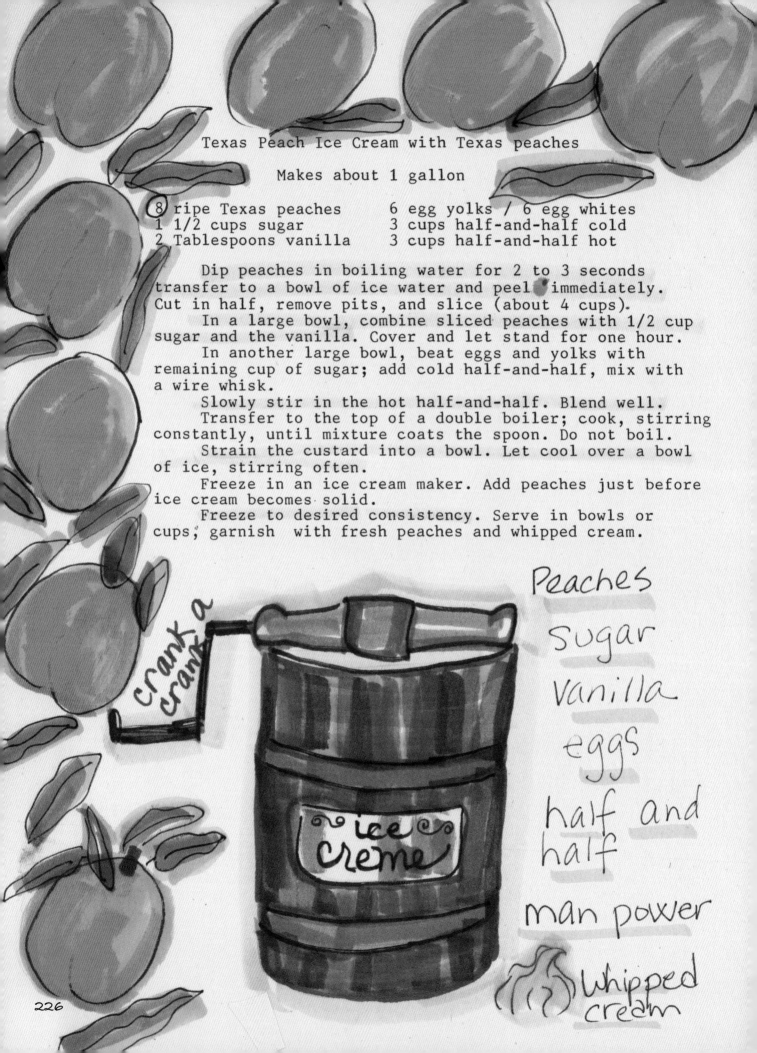

Texas Peach Ice Cream with Texas peaches

Makes about 1 gallon

8 ripe Texas peaches   6 egg yolks / 6 egg whites
1 1/2 cups sugar   3 cups half-and-half cold
2 Tablespoons vanilla   3 cups half-and-half hot

Dip peaches in boiling water for 2 to 3 seconds transfer to a bowl of ice water and peel immediately. Cut in half, remove pits, and slice (about 4 cups).

In a large bowl, combine sliced peaches with 1/2 cup sugar and the vanilla. Cover and let stand for one hour.

In another large bowl, beat eggs and yolks with remaining cup of sugar; add cold half-and-half, mix with a wire whisk.

Slowly stir in the hot half-and-half. Blend well.

Transfer to the top of a double boiler; cook, stirring constantly, until mixture coats the spoon. Do not boil.

Strain the custard into a bowl. Let cool over a bowl of ice, stirring often.

Freeze in an ice cream maker. Add peaches just before ice cream becomes solid.

Freeze to desired consistency. Serve in bowls or cups; garnish with fresh peaches and whipped cream.

crank a crank

ice creme

Peaches
sugar
Vanilla
eggs
half and half
man power
Whipped cream

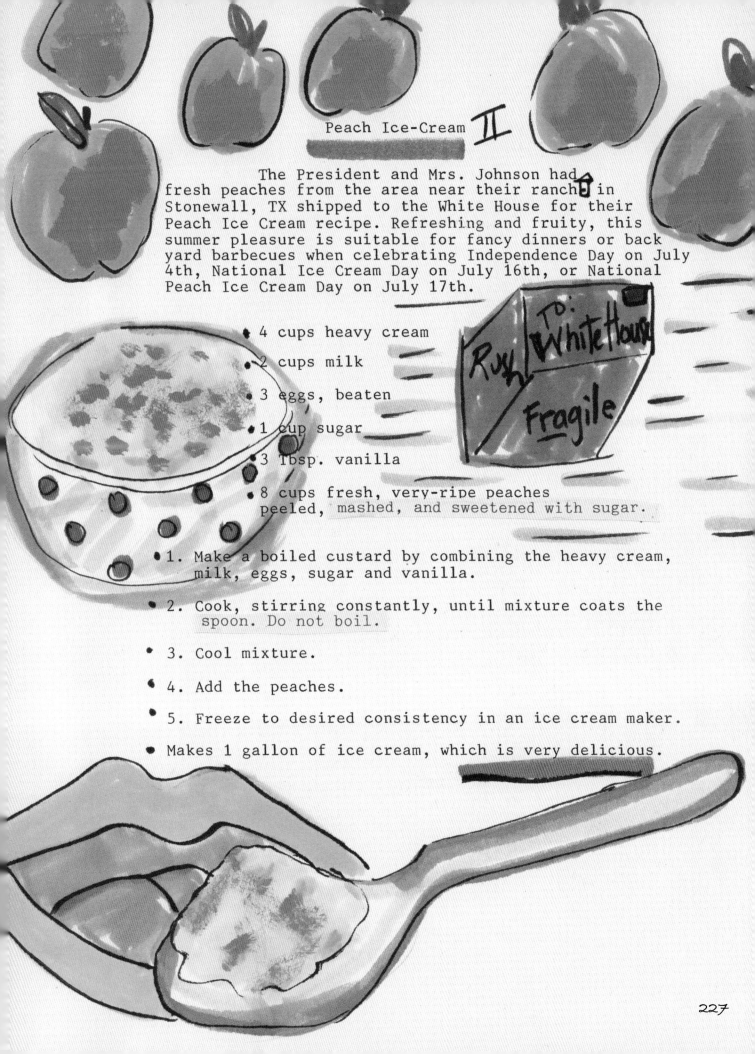

Peach Ice-Cream II

The President and Mrs. Johnson had fresh peaches from the area near their ranch in Stonewall, TX shipped to the White House for their Peach Ice Cream recipe. Refreshing and fruity, this summer pleasure is suitable for fancy dinners or back yard barbecues when celebrating Independence Day on July 4th, National Ice Cream Day on July 16th, or National Peach Ice Cream Day on July 17th.

- 4 cups heavy cream
- 2 cups milk
- 3 eggs, beaten
- 1 cup sugar
- 3 Tbsp. vanilla
- 8 cups fresh, very-ripe peaches peeled, mashed, and sweetened with sugar.

1. Make a boiled custard by combining the heavy cream, milk, eggs, sugar and vanilla.

2. Cook, stirring constantly, until mixture coats the spoon. Do not boil.

3. Cool mixture.

4. Add the peaches.

5. Freeze to desired consistency in an ice cream maker.

Makes 1 gallon of ice cream, which is very delicious.

227

MERINGUE PARK

This dessert was served at the KOREA DINNER on May 17, 1965. It was the perfect dessert to finish off a menu that included: Cold Baby Lobster White House, Fillet of Beef California, Potatoes Empire, Bibb Lettuce Salad, and Gourmandise Cheese.

5 egg whites	Pinch of salt
3/4 cup granulated sugar	1/4 cup confectioners' sugar
1 teaspoon vanilla extract	2 cups chilled heavy cream
2 tablespoons confectioners sugar	
2 cups sweetened sliced fresh peaches	

Heat oven to 250F. Beat egg whites and salt together until stiff; gradually add granulated sugar and beat until stiff. Fold the 1/4 cup confectioners' sugar and vanilla into meringue. Grease large baking sheets and line with wax paper. Trace 4 eight inch circles on wax paper and grease (leave 2 inches between circles). Spread one quarter of the meringue in each circle. Bake meringues for 45 minutes, or until lightly browned. Turn off heat and leave in oven until cold. Carefully peel paper off meringues. Whip cream and the 2 tablespoons confectioners sugar until stiff; divide in half. Fold drained peaches into half of the cream. Place a meringue layer on serving plate and spread with 1/3 of the peach cream mixture. Repeat layers twice and top with remaining meringue. Spread most of remaining cream around sides of cake. Spoon leftover cream in a cake-decorating bag with a star tip and garnish.
Serves 8

NOTE: MERINGUE CIRCLES MUST BE SMOOTHED FLAT TO STACK.

W.H.I.P.P.E.D

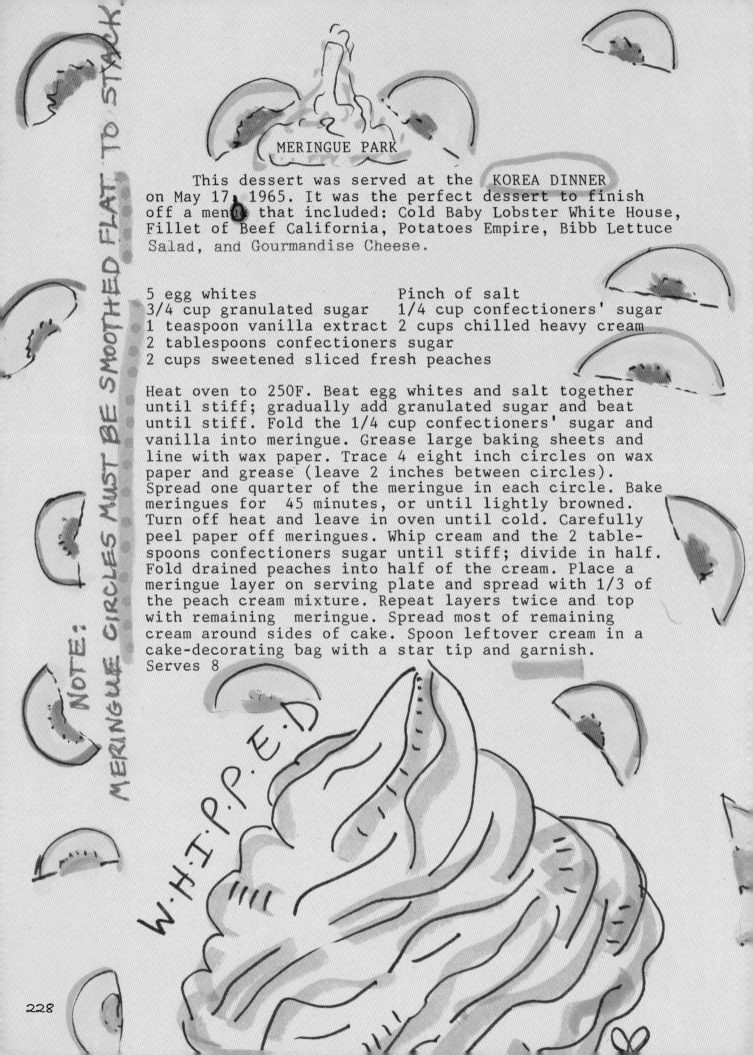

Lady Bird's world Famous Lemon Cake

3/4 cup butter	1 1/4 cups sugar
8 egg yolks	2 1/2 cups sifted flour
3 tsp. baking powder	1/2 tsp. salt
3/4 cup milk	1 tsp. vanilla
1 tsp. grated lemon peel	1 tsp. fresh lemon juice

In a large bowl, cream butter and sugar until light and fluffy.
In a seperate bowl beat egg yolks until light and lemon colored. Gradually add to butter and sugar and mix with beater just enough to mix.
Sift together flour, baking powder, and salt. Resift. Add sifted ingredients to butter, sugar, egg yolk mix. Mix and slowly add milk. Add vanilla, grated lemon peel and lemon juice. Beat two minutes.
Bake in a greased and floured Bundt pan at 325F for one hour or until toothpick inserted in cake comes out clean.
Cool in pan for 10-15 minutes, turn out on rack and sprinkle top of cake with powdered sugar.

Perfect-o!

Pecan pie
SOUTHERN

* Southern Pecan Pie

1 cup brown sugar
2 tablespoons flour
1 tablespoon butter
1 cup corn syrup
3 beaten eggs
1 teaspoon vanilla
1/4 teaspoon salt
1 cup pecan halves

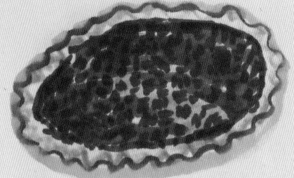

Mix sugar and flour. Cream with butter. Add syrup
and eggs. Beat well. Add vanilla, salt and nuts.
Pour into an unbaked pastry shell.
Bake for 30 minutes in a moderate-slow oven (325)
or until mixture is set.

VIP PIE BAKING

PEACH COBBLER
1987 Stonewall Peach Jamboree
1st Prize

Lillie's

BOTTOM CRUST:

2 cups flour
1/4 cup sugar
1/2 tsp. salt

1 stick butter
1/2 cup lard
2 Tbsp. cold water

Mix flour, sugar and salt, add butter and lard and blend until crumbly.
Add water and mix with a fork. Then knead dough 3 or 4 times (no more). Divide in half, roll out on floured surface, cut in strips and put strips in bottom of a good and greasy 8x8 pan. Put other half of dough in ziplock bag in refrigerator or freezer for future use

TOP CRUST

3 cups flour
1/4 cup sugar
1 tsp salt

1 cup Crisco
1 egg plus water to make 1/2 cup

Mix flour, sugar and salt, add Crisco and blend until crumbly. Add egg and water, stir with fork until mixture gathers into a ball. Divide in half and roll out for top crust. Put other half in ziplock bag for future use.

4 cups fresh Stonewall Peaches, sliced
3/4 cup sugar (or sweeten to taste)
1 Tbls. butter

Add sugar to peaches and heat, but do not boil. Pour this over pastry strips in an 8 X 8 pan. Dot with butter. Cover with top crust; poke holes in crust with fork. Sprinkle with sugar and cinnamon. Bake at 400 degrees for 30 minutes. (It's always nice to have the extra crusts in the fridge or freezer for a quick cobbler.

JANE DAUGHERTY

BLUE RIBBON AWARD!

Spa Crepes

1 large egg
2 egg whites
1 1/4 cup nonfat skim milk
3/4 cup stone-ground whole wheat pastry flour
1/4 cup unbleached flour
2 tablespoons toasted wheat germ
1 1/2 tablespoons vegetable oil
1 teaspoon cinnamon
1/2 teaspoon vanilla extract

In blender combine all ingredients and mix
one minute. Pour into another container, cover
and let batter stand at room temperature at
least 1 hour. (NOTE: Consistency of batter
should be no thicker than heavy cream)

In lightly greased 6 inch crepe pan (non-stick)
over medium heat, pour in 3 tablespoons batter
and quickly tilt pan in all directions until
batter is evenly distributed.

Cook until underside is golden, about 30 seconds,
turn, and cook the other side 20 seconds.
Cook until all the batter is used, greasing pan
only when necessary. Stack crepes in batches of
8.

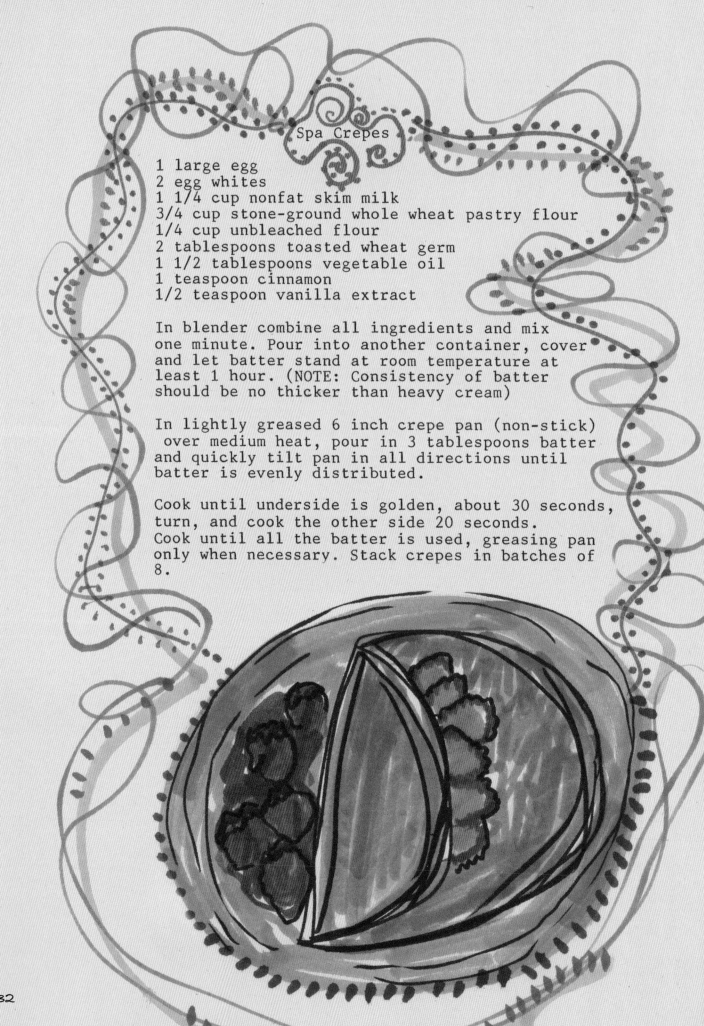

Sauce Anglaise au Kirsch

Egg yolks   Kirsch or light rum
Sugar   Vanilla Extract
Milk

In top of double boiler, combine 5 eggs yolks
and 1/3 cup sugar. Stir in 2 cups scalded milk. Mix
well with wire whip. Cook over hot water, stirring,
about 15 minutes, or until sauce thickens enough to
coat the spoon. Add 2 tablespoons Kirsch and 1 teaspoon
vanilla extract and stir again. Serve with lemon souffle.
Makes 3 cups.

Chef Haller's Lemon Souffle

This is baked in a shallow oval casserole.
It has more crust and everybody loves more crust!!

Butter   Salt
Flour   Eggs
Milk   Sugar
Grated lemon rind

Grease and place a 3-inch foil collar around a 2-quart
oval souffle dish. Sprinkle dish lightly with sugar
and set aside.
In a large saucepan, melt 1/3 cup butter. Add 1/2 cup
cup flour and stir to form a paste. Gradually stir in
1 1/2 cups scalded milk, cook 2 to 3 minutes or until
mixture is thickened and smooth. Add 1/3 cup sugar
and 1/4 teaspoon salt and mix again. Remove from heat
and add 8 egg yolks, adding one at a time, mixing well
after each addition. Stir in 2 tablespoons grated lemon
rind. Beat 8 egg whites until foamy. Stir in 2 tablespoons
sugar and continue beating until stiff, but not dry.
Gently fold egg white into flour-egg batter. Spoon
mixture into prepared souffle dish. Bake in pre-heated
(375 degree) oven 45 minutes or until golden brown and
puffy. Serve immediately with sauce Anglaise au kirsch.

Peanuts!

Mrs. Lyndon B. Johnson's Recipe for Peanut Brittle----

- 1 1/2 cups sugar
- 1/2 cup water
- 1/2 cup white Karo
- 1 1/2 cups peanuts (raw or parched)
- 1 heaping TBS. butter
- 1/2 tsp. salt
- 1/2 tsp. soda

Peanut Brittle

Cook first 3 ingredients in large skillet until the mixture forms a hard ball in cold water. Add peanuts. Cook until a rich golden brown, stirring constantly.

Add butter, salt and soda together, Stir batch and quickly pour into buttered pans. Let harden.

Mrs. Lyndon B. Johnson's Recipe for Wheaties Coconut Cookies

- 1 tsp. soda
- 1/2 tsp. baking powder
- 1/2 tsp. vanilla
- 2 cups Wheaties
- 1 cup half shortening, half butter
- 1 cup brown sugar
- 1 cup white sugar
- 2 eggs, beaten
- 2 cups coconut
- 2 cups flour

Sift and measure flour. Add soda, baking powder and salt and sift again. Blend shortening/butter into flour mixture and beat with mixer. Add brown sugar, white sugar and eggs and beat well. By hand stir in coconut. Drop by teaspoons on greased cookie sheet and cook at 350F until lightly brown, about 12 minutes.

Cookies for champions!

WHEATIES

234

Lady Bird's Strawberry Icebox Pie

1 17-oz. pkg. marshmallows

2 cups fresh strawberries
   or 1 box frozen, sweetened

1 cup whipping cream

1 baked 9-inch pastry shell

Put marshmallows in double boiler. Add 2 tbs. of strawberry juice. Cook until marshmallows are melted. Mix strawberries and marshmallows thoroughly. Chill about 2 hours. Fold whipped cream into marshmallow mixture and pour into baked pastry shell. Chill until firm.

Pecan Pralines

This is THE recipe used in making pralines sold to all the Mexican restaurants in Austin. Individually wrapped in cellophane, the pralines traveled well.

4 3/4 cup sugar

4 cups pecans (halves or large pieces)

2 cups water

1/8 tsp. salt

2 Tbsp. butter

Put 4 cups of the sugar, pecans, water and salt in a pan and bring to a boil; meanwhile, melt ¾ cup sugar in an iron skillet and let it brown slightly but not scorch. When it is caramel colored, pour it into the first mixture. Cook until it forms a firm ball when dropped in cold water. Put waxed paper over newspaper laid out on flat surface. Add butter and beat until mixture cools a little. Then drop by spoonsful (any size desired) on the waxed paper. When the pralines are cool they will be hard and will lift easily off the paper.

Harry Truman loved getting these and always asked for a "few" more to give to the Madam.

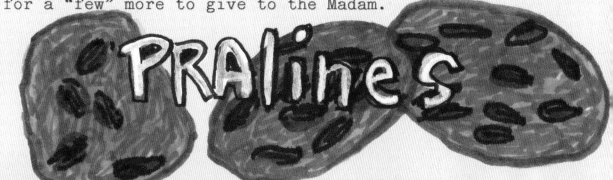

PRESIDENT JOHNSON'S FAVORITE
DOUBLE DIVINITY FUDGE—A TREASURED
FAMILY RECIPE

2 cups sugar
2/3 cup water
1/2 cup light corn syrup
1 tsp. vanilla

2 egg whites, slightly
    beaten
dash salt (added to egg
    whites)

    Combine 1/2 cup sugar and 1/3 cup water;
cook to 240F or until small amount of syrup forms
a ball in cold water. Separately, cook remaining
1 1/2 cups sugar, 1/3 cup water, and corn syrup
until it forms a hard ball (250F). Let first syrup
cool slightly. Add slowly to egg whites, beating
constantly, about 1 to 2 minutes, or until mixture
loses its gloss; add second syrup the same way. Add
vanilla and turn out into greased pan. Cut in squares
when cold.

GRAPENUTS PUDDING

3 cups milk, scalded
3/4 cup sugar
2 eggs, beaten
1/4 tsp. nutmeg, divided

pinch salt
1 tsp vanilla
1/2 cup Grapenuts cereal
1/2 cup raisins, or
    another 1/2 cup Grapenuts

Mix all ingredients except 1/8 tsp nutmeg in an ovenproof mixing
bowl. Place bowl of pudding in a pan of water and bake for about
one hour in a 350F oven. Remove from oven and sprinkle remaining
nutmeg on top.
Serves 8.

SOUFFLE GRAND MARNIER

8 egg yolks, lightly beaten
2/3 cup sugar
1/2 cup plus a shot of Grand Marnier liqueur

10 egg whites, beaten
1/4 tsp. cream of tartar

Preheat oven to 400F. Beat in a double boiler over boiling water
the egg yolks and sugar. Continue to beat until the mixture forms
a broad ribbon as it runs from a spoon. Add the liqueur. To
arrest cooking, transfer the mixture to a bowl and beat over ice
until cooled. Beat the egg whites until foamy. Add cream of
tartar and continue to beat until stiff, but not dry. Fold the
egg yolk mixture into the whites and mound the mixture in a
souffle dish. Bake 12 to 15 minutes, until firm, and serve at
once. Serves 10.

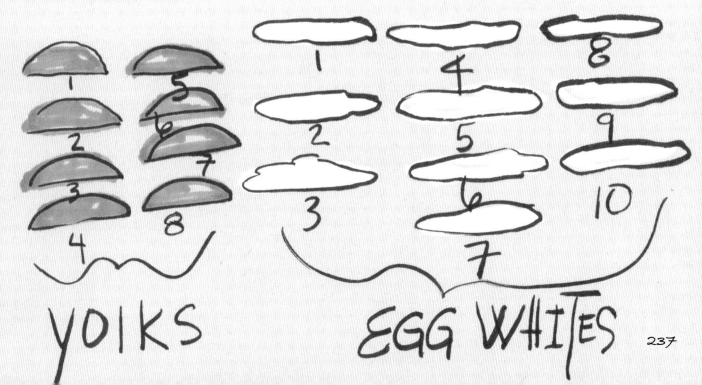

YOLKS   EGG WHITES

Christmas

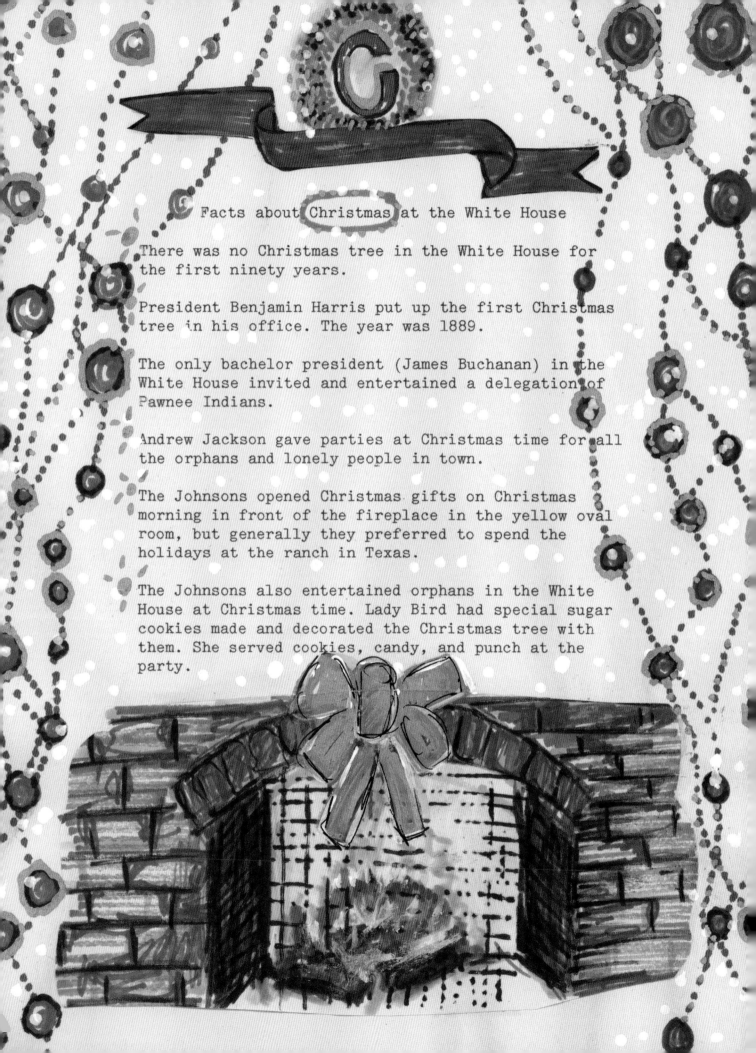

Facts about Christmas at the White House

There was no Christmas tree in the White House for the first ninety years.

President Benjamin Harris put up the first Christmas tree in his office. The year was 1889.

The only bachelor president (James Buchanan) in the White House invited and entertained a delegation of Pawnee Indians.

Andrew Jackson gave parties at Christmas time for all the orphans and lonely people in town.

The Johnsons opened Christmas gifts on Christmas morning in front of the fireplace in the yellow oval room, but generally they preferred to spend the holidays at the ranch in Texas.

The Johnsons also entertained orphans in the White House at Christmas time. Lady Bird had special sugar cookies made and decorated the Christmas tree with them. She served cookies, candy, and punch at the party.

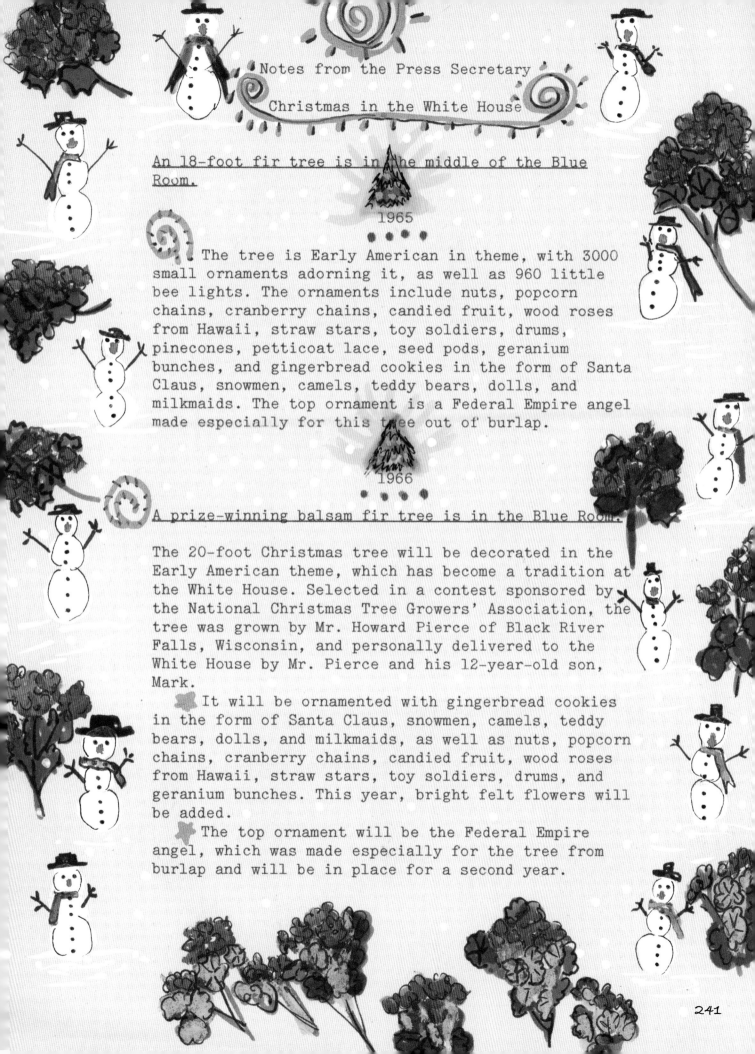

Notes from the Press Secretary

Christmas in the White House

<u>An 18-foot fir tree is in the middle of the Blue Room.</u>

1965

••••

The tree is Early American in theme, with 3000 small ornaments adorning it, as well as 960 little bee lights. The ornaments include nuts, popcorn chains, cranberry chains, candied fruit, wood roses from Hawaii, straw stars, toy soldiers, drums, pinecones, petticoat lace, seed pods, geranium bunches, and gingerbread cookies in the form of Santa Claus, snowmen, camels, teddy bears, dolls, and milkmaids. The top ornament is a Federal Empire angel made especially for this tree out of burlap.

1966

••••

<u>A prize-winning balsam fir tree is in the Blue Room.</u>

The 20-foot Christmas tree will be decorated in the Early American theme, which has become a tradition at the White House. Selected in a contest sponsored by the National Christmas Tree Growers' Association, the tree was grown by Mr. Howard Pierce of Black River Falls, Wisconsin, and personally delivered to the White House by Mr. Pierce and his 12-year-old son, Mark.

It will be ornamented with gingerbread cookies in the form of Santa Claus, snowmen, camels, teddy bears, dolls, and milkmaids, as well as nuts, popcorn chains, cranberry chains, candied fruit, wood roses from Hawaii, straw stars, toy soldiers, drums, and geranium bunches. This year, bright felt flowers will be added.

The top ornament will be the Federal Empire angel, which was made especially for the tree from burlap and will be in place for a second year.

241

CHISTMAS IN THE WHITE HOUSE

1967

A 16-foot, 6 inch blue spruce tree in the Blue Room is trimmed in the Early American theme that has become a tradition at the White House. Ohio won the right to furnish this year's tree in a competition sponsored by the National Christmas Tree Growers' Association. This year's tree was grown by Mrs. Howard M. Cowan of Portage County.

Decorations on the tree include gingerbread cookies in the shape of snowmen, camels, teddy bears, dolls, and milkmaids; nuts, popcorn, and cranberry chains; candied fruit, wood roses from Hawaii, straw stars, toy soldiers, drums, geranium bunches, bright felt flowers, dried seed pods and leaves, and yarn bows. This year shiny silver balls, silver stars, and small round mirrors will be added, and elves will be placed under the tree. The top ornament is the Federal Empire angel which was made especially for the tree from burlap.

1968

The 20-foot white pine displayed in the Blue Room was chosen by Mr. Don Goodwin of Indianapolis, Indiana. His entry in the National Christmas Tree Growers' Association, Inc. competition won Indiana the right to furnish the White House tree for 1968. The tree was grown in Osgood, Indiana, at the Gala Sheets tree farm, and was delivered to the White House Friday, December 13, by Mr. and Mrs. Goodwin.

The tree is decorated in the Early American theme, a tradition at the White House. Ornaments include gingerbread cookies in the shape of snowmen, camels, teddy bears, dolls, and milkmaids, as well as nuts, popcorn chains, cranberry chains, candied fruit, straw stars, toy soldiers, drums, and geranium bunches. Other ornaments include bright felt flowers, dried seed pods and leaves, strings of tiny mirrors, and gold foil sunbursts. The top ornament will be an angel which was made for the tree four years ago.

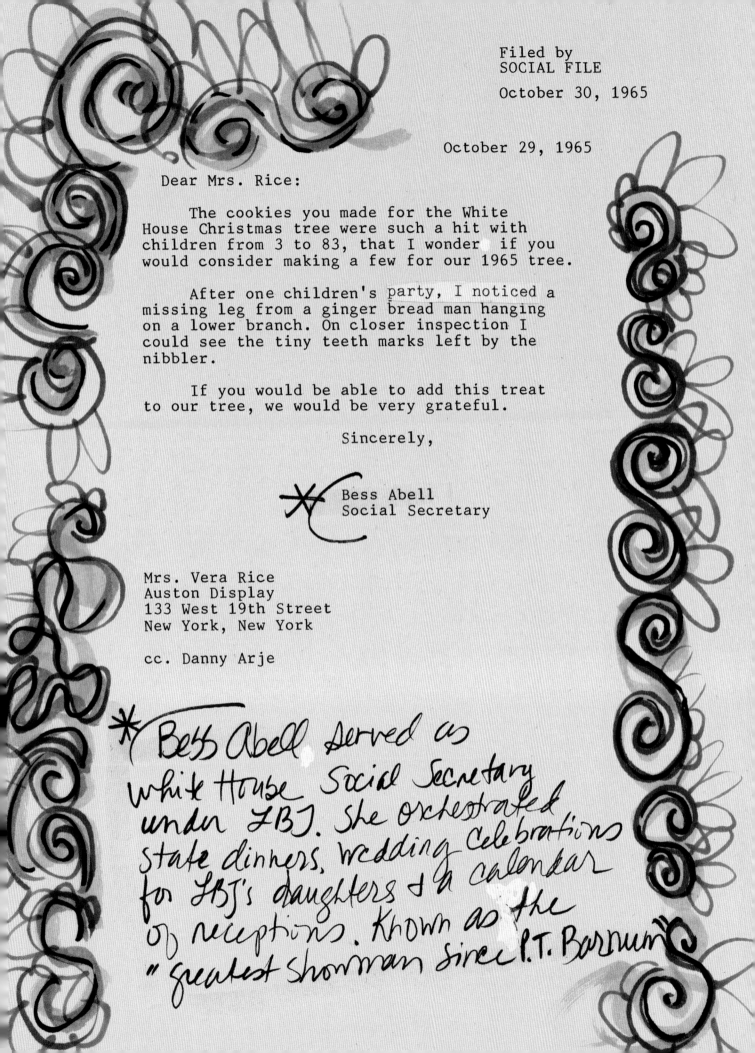

October 29, 1965

Dear Mrs. Rice:

The cookies you made for the White
House Christmas tree were such a hit with
children from 3 to 83, that I wonder if you
would consider making a few for our 1965 tree.

After one children's party, I noticed a
missing leg from a ginger bread man hanging
on a lower branch. On closer inspection I
could see the tiny teeth marks left by the
nibbler.

If you would be able to add this treat
to our tree, we would be very grateful.

Sincerely,

Bess Abell
Social Secretary

Mrs. Vera Rice
Auston Display
133 West 19th Street
New York, New York

cc. Danny Arje

*Bess Abell served as
white House Social Secretary
under LBJ. She orchestrated
state dinners, wedding celebrations
for LBJ's daughters + a calendar
of receptions. Known as the
"greatest showman since P.T. Barnum"

In 1967 Lady Bird received a letter asking what was on her menu for Christmas dinner.

Lady Bird replied:

"Christmas dinner will be traditional favorites of both Thanksgiving and Christmas, with turkey and an additional platter of wild turkey, cornbread dressing, string beans with almonds, sweet potatoes and marshmallows, hot homemade rolls, cranberry salad, ambrosia, fruitcake, and angel food cake."

She added that a "handcrafted, live wreath, a gift of the Northern Cheyenne Indians of Montana, will also be used as part of the decorations."

In 1968 Lady Bird received another letter asking what was on her Christmas menu. It was similar to the menu of the previous year, with a few tweaks.

Lady Bird replied:

"Chef Henry Haller is preparing our traditional Christmas menu. Favorites will include
Oyster cocktail
Roast turkey with giblet gravy
Cornbread dressing
Beans with toasted almonds
Bibb lettuce salad
Cranberry sauce
Homemade sweet rolls
Homemade fruitcake
Ambrosia
Eggnog

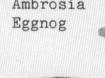

A favorite Christmas gift to Lady Bird was from
Mr. and Mrs. Charles W. Engelhard of Far Hills,
New Jersey. It was an 18th century Italian Creche
(nativity scene).

The creche consisted of 30 baroque carved figures
including the holy family, the three kings and
their attendants, beautiful shepherds, angels,
cherubs, and the various animals associated with
the manger scene. Brightly colored and richly
clothed, the figures were from 12 to 18 inches
high and were carved from wood by Marisa Piccole
Catello of Naples, Italy.

Lady Bird loved this gift and treasured it for
many years.

Mrs. Engelhard (Jane) was a noted supporter of
White House restorations. She assisted Jacqueline
Kennedy in redecorating the White House and
served on committees to preserve and restore the
White House during every presidential
administration from John F. Kennedy to George W.
Bush.

245

WINE CUP
Callirhoe involucrata

TEXAS WILDFLOWERS

Four nerve Daisy
"the perky sue"
Hymenoxys scaposa

Prarie Verbena
Glandularia Bipinnatifida

Goldeneye Phlox
Phlox roemeriana

Large Buttercup
Ranunculus macranthus

Bibliography

Cannon, Poppy and Brooks, Patricia. The Presidents' Cookbook. New York: Bonanza Books, 1967

Clifford, Marnie. Washington Cook Book

Erwin, Jane. The White House Cookbook. Follett Publishing, 1964

Fields, Alonzo. My 21 years in the White House. New York: Bard-McCann, Inc. 1961

Gillette, Fannie. White House Cookbook. 1925

Haller, Henry with Aronson, Virginia. The White House Family Cookbook. New York: Random House, 1987

Jones, Robert. The President's Own Cookbook. Culinary Arts Institute, 1972.

Kimbell, Marie. "The Epicure of the White House", Virginia Quarterly Review. January 1933

Kimball, Marie. The Martha Washington Cookbook. New York Bard-McCann, Inc. 1940

Verdon, Rene. White House Chef Cookbook, New York: Doubleday

Treasury of White House Recipes. New York: McGraw-Hill 1973

The American Heritage Cookbook. New York: American Publishing Company, 1964

Smith, Marie. Entertaining in the White House. Washington D.C. Hollis Books, 1967

Jetton, Walter, with Arthur Whitman. The LBJ Barbeque Cookbook. New York: Pocket Books, 1965